I0748487

LOVING WISDOM
A Second Collection Of Stories That Nourish The Soul

By The Wisdom Whisperers:

Malena Cunningham Anderson

Henrietta Stith Andrews

Leslie Hazle Bussey

La Verne C. Dixon

Joan Wagnon Drescher

Frances Johnson Dunston

Joyce Coleman Edwards

Nina R. Hickson

Lolita Browning Jackson

Roberta Jackson

Tisa Jackson

Rosalyn Roberts Mack

Beatrice Hunter Pack

E. Paulette Smith-Epps

Gail Tusan Washington

OVERFLOW BOOKS

LOVING WISDOM
A Second Collection Of Stories That Nourish The Soul

Co-Authors: Malena Cunningham Anderson, Henrietta Stith Andrews, Leslie Hazle Bussey, La Verne C. Dixon, Joan Wagnon Drescher, Frances Johnson Dunston, Joyce Coleman Edwards, Nina R. Hickson, Lolita Browning Jackson, Roberta Jackson, Tisa Jackson, Rosalyn Roberts Mack, Beatrice Hunter Pack, E. Paulette Smith-Epps, Gail Tusan Washington

Copyright © 2023 All rights reserved

Published by Overflow Books an Imprint of Spirit Filled Creations (Chesapeake, Va.)
www.SpiritFilledCreations.com

No part of this book may be reproduced or transmitted by any person or entity, including internet search engines and retailers, in any form or by any means, electronic or mechanical, including photocopying, recording, scanning or by any information storage and retrieval system without the prior written permission of the author of this book.

This anthology reflects the various author's present recollections of experiences over time. Some names and characteristics have been written, some events have been compressed, and some dialogue has been recreated. The advice and strategies found within may not be suitable for every situation. This work is sold with the understanding that neither the author's nor the publisher are held responsible for the results accrued from the advice in this book.

Scriptures marked NIV are taken from the NEW INTERNATIONAL VERSION (NIV): Scripture taken from THE HOLY BIBLE, NEW INTERNATIONAL VERSION ®. Copyright© 1973, 1978, 1984, 2011 by Biblica, Inc. TM. Used by permission of Zondervan. Scriptures marked KJV are taken from the KING JAMES VERSION (KJV): KING JAMES VERSION, public domain.

International Standard Book Number: 978-1-7342948-9-7

Hardcover First Edition

Printed in the United States of America

Read What Reviewers Have To Say About This Second Collection Of Loving Wisdom.

Loving Wisdom, A Second Collection of Stories to Nourish the Soul, evokes the choices I have made during my life in my struggle toward success. In this collection of essays and prose, these women of achievement draw us close to the heart and the soul of their unique journeys.

Dr. Althea Natalga Sumpter, Researcher, Scholar, and Ethnographer

Congratulations to the Wisdom Whisperers for accomplishing what few have — a literary gem that underscores the strength and vulnerability of what it means to be a woman. Well done!

Imani Monica McCullough
Author, *When I Was Broken* and Founder, YANASISTERS (You are Not Alone)

Loving Wisdom, A Second Collection of Stories that Nourish the Soul, is an empowering and poignant memoir that chronicles the authors' remarkable journeys of survival and triumph over seemingly insurmountable obstacles. This book's raw honesty and vulnerability take readers on a rollercoaster of emotions, from despair to hope, as they navigate through unimaginable challenges. Through their stories, readers are inspired to believe in the resilience of the human spirit and find solace in the power of perseverance. This book is a powerful reminder of our innate ability to overcome adversity and find strength in the most extraordinary circumstances.

Elizabeth Espy, Author, *Choice Mom, Loving Wisdom*

The power of women to cure, to love, to lift, and to heal is evident in these pages. These powerful testimonies will pull at your heartstrings and inspire you to recognize the gifts that others have given you and the gifts you have to give. This collection of women whispering the wisdom gained by their victories and scars is a labor of love.

Bensonetta Tipton Lane, Retired Judge
Author, *Letting Go, Loving Wisdom*

As a former trial lawyer (prosecutor and later criminal defense lawyer), I am glad, Judge Tusan, you became a judge-smart, fair, good listener.

Elaine McGruder, Retired Attorney

When outstanding women share their life experiences, it makes for an extraordinary read. Bravo to these brave women who cared enough to share with us.

Lois Carrington Tusan, Retired Educator
Author, *A Teacher's Gift, Loving Wisdom*

The eloquent prologue lovingly says, "We whisper truth." In reality, these women shout truth to the rafters in a way that not only captures the reader but gives glory to God and the village of women we admire and cherish. The authors weave personal experiences encompassing adversity and triumph, which speak to the soul. Ultimately, the stories inspire and nurture us through the powerful words and actions of devout women in our community.

Kirby Roy III
Screenwriter/Author, *Destiny's Grace, The Void of Lies, Two Roads and Love Letters*

In this revealing chronicle, women share their wisdom via the most intimate stories about the complexities of their lives. Each one battles the odds, displaying bold grit and determination to reach a personal goal to become a parent, serve as a caregiver, or meet other life challenges. For some, the circumstances they ultimately overcome may appear insurmountable. But they are winners in the true sense of the word; they "keep on keeping on," mounting a "never give up" attitude and often "letting go and letting God" take control. Their words send both inspirational and powerful messages to the reader.

Mary M. Jessie
Retired Educator/Human Resources Consultant

Loving Wisdom, a Second Collection of Stories that Nourish the Soul, encourages readers to listen to the still, small voice in their inner being. Doing so enables one to release stress, think boldly, and gain serenity.

Earl Menchhofer
Author, *Stay in the Game - Seven Steps to Serenity*

This compilation of personal essays by extraordinary women demonstrates how life teaches us what we need to know if we pay attention. This collection of wisdom rivals anything you might read in the great spiritual books like the Bible, the Tao, the Quran, or the Bhagavad Gita.

Dr. James O. Rodgers
Business adviser and spiritual teacher; Co-Author, *Diversity Training That Generates Real Change and Managing Differently,* and Author, *Epiphany: Finding Truth without Losing Faith*

When God has called upon you to take care of another, you will soon find out that every day, either you will touch their life, or their life will touch yours. And you'll both be the better for it.

Justice Leah Ward Sears (retired)
Georgia Supreme Court

Wisdom whispered should never be taken lightly. To hear a whisper, we must focus, listen, and receive what is truly being said. Our understanding deepens, and our strength renews as we listen to one another.

Loving Wisdom is a special collective that reminds me to share knowledge and experiences and that our intimacy begins inside of us. Perspectives, triumphs, and lessons come from living. The Whisperers' powerful testimonies ignited me to testify!

Kym Webster, Hila the Healer
Spiritual/Natural Healing
3Doves Healing, LLC

Honest, insightful, and inspiring, Loving Wisdom, is an engaging collection of essays and poems, full of compelling personal stories that gracefully cover a range of topics from the loss of a loved one to overcoming professional and personal challenges. The wisdom and perspective whispered throughout this book, resonate deeply and provide invaluable lessons for living.

Omar L. Douglass
Poet and Author, *No Disclaimers*

Meet The Wisdom Whisperers

Malena Cunningham Anderson

Henrietta Stith Andrews

Leslie Hazle Bussey

La Verne C. Dixon

Joan Wagnon Drescher

Frances Johnson Dunston

Joyce Coleman Edwards

Nina R. Hickson

Lolita Browning Jackson

Roberta Jackson

Tisa Jackson

Rosalyn Roberts Mack

Beatrice Hunter Pack

E. Paulette Smith-Epps

Gail Tusan Washington

Loving Wisdom
A Second Collection of Stories That Nourish the Soul

Acknowledgments

On these pages, the Wisdom Whisperers express their gratitude for the bountiful reservoirs of wisdom that guided them through their times of challenge.

They recognize the legacy of values and courage bestowed upon them by their ancestors and loved ones who preceded them. They pay homage to family and friends who supported and comforted them at critical times. They honor the love and nurture of their sister Whisperers, who enabled them to share their stories of Loving Wisdom.

They allow us the privilege of insight into the generation of this beautiful collection of life stories.

Frances Johnson Dunston

Henrietta Stith Andrews

I want to thank Reverends Lorraine McNeal, Renee Jackson, and my daughter Cathy Andrews for reading early drafts. Thank you to Rev. Joann Broten for the conversations that clarified details about our work as Associate Conference Ministers. Thank you to Benni Lane for her insightful editing that brought laughter in response to one of her suggestions. Thank you to my Spiritual Director, Sr. Rachelle Harper, for her encouragement, over the years, to draft my stories, woven into this chapter, which guided me toward ministry. Finally, I want to thank Rev. Dr. Donald Freemen, posthumously, who is not mentioned by name in my chapter but whose wisdom, as my counselor and seminary professor, was significant to my journey toward ordained ministry.

Leslie Hazle Bussey

I have the wild, great fortune to love and be/have been loved by many women who, in addition to my mom, Lydia, have been chosen mothers, sisters, and whisperers of truth and hope into me. The Great Women of my life are my godmother, Pilar Wells, and my grandmother, Hazel Hazle, whose presence is no longer on this physical earth but whose spirits and wisdom live in my bones, in the timbre of my voice, in the time I allow between my reaction and my response. They would have been kindred spirits if they'd known one another – both loved words, were astonishingly brave, and embodied an exquisite balance of femininity and impervious strength. I like to think of myself as a vessel carrying forward their energy and dedicate my first foray into poetry to them: brave, strong, vulnerable, hopeful, and loving.

La Verne C. Dixon

I dedicate this essay to my family, especially my baby girl, Rachael Williams, and her "crew." Also, my beloved church, my pastor, and especially the Diaconate Board for praying me back to life. A special thank you to Deacon Vernita Freeman and Grady Hospital medics Allison Schwartz and Joel Jacob, who worked hard to make my heart beat.

Joan Wagnon Drescher

I thank my brother, John Wagnon, and fellow Wisdom Whisperer, Benni Tipton Lane, for their encouragement, support, and awesome editing help with my essay. Also, many thanks to Gail for asking me to be a part of this incredible group of ladies and giving me the opportunity to share my personal story.

Joyce Coleman Edwards

I'd like to thank my fellow Wisdom Whisperers for having the courage to do this again. We learned so much from our first book, and so many people were encouraged by it. I thank my husband for always holding me up, keeping me grounded, and being the wind that keeps me in flight. And finally, I thank God for keeping me sane during my darkest hour and letting me be happy again. To Him be the glory!

Lolita Browning Jackson

To my parents, the late QV and Marie Browning, thank you for teaching me to believe in myself. Because of you, I am blessed to know what being loved truly feels like. To my siblings Elma, Calvin, Belinda, Quinton, Sylvia, Duvale, Darryl, and our beloved angel in Heaven, Cindy, I thank you all for reminding me what it means to be a village and showing me daily what support looks like. No one does it like us! I love you all! To the love of my life, my husband, John Michael Jackson, thank you for seeing me, hearing me, loving me, valuing me, and always having my back. My father would be pleased. To my son, Aaron, thank you for changing my life. Becoming your mother is the best part of being me. To Gail Tusan, thank you for inviting me to be a part of this magnificent project and encouraging me to share my story. Love, Lolita

Roberta Jackson

I thank God for my mother, Frankie Keepler Robertson; without her, I would not be here, and I wouldn't have so many wisdom nuggets to share from our journey as mother and daughter. I thank Gail for this opportunity to share, encourage, and even inspire...the second time is a charm! To the Faithful Four – Tyrone (husband), Tommie (son), Isaac (son), Vickie (sister), and the rest of my village of family and friends. Thank you.

Thank you for your endless support, love, belief, and truthfulness throughout the years. I appreciate you and love you to life. God Bless!

Tisa Jackson

To my mommy, who was my champion at the onset of my alopecia journey. I would not have been as brave without your wings always lifting me up. To my husband, Andrew, who loves me for me. Thank you for always making me feel beautiful and staying on me about eating right. To my children, Kai, Drew, and Davis, always supporting and encouraging their mama. To my grandson Tai, for reminding me that the small moments are the stuff of life! And to all my family and friends, thank you for being such uplifting and inspirational forces in my life.

"Love who you are, embrace who you are. When you love yourself, people pick up on that; they see confidence and self-esteem and naturally gravitate towards you." ~ Lilly Singh

Rosalyn Roberts Mack

I dedicate this essay to all women who have experienced or are experiencing challenges resulting from complications during pregnancy and childbirth. I honor their strength and pray that their healthcare needs are met with compassion, competence, and respect. Hearing their stories made me reflect on my unpredictable childbirth experience, and I was strengthened, renewed, and inspired to share my wisdom with others through writing my essay.
I thank Bensonetta Tipton Lane, my editing partner, for asking probing questions and providing candid feedback, which helped me

authentically tell my story. I thank my husband, Trentton K. Mack, the love of my life, key supporter, and devoted editor of our story; our daughter, Victoria, for lifting us up during our difficult days and helping us cope with our loss more than she will ever know; our son Joshua for his editorial review of our story; and the medical community who took such good care of our physical, emotional and spiritual needs when we needed it most.

Beatrice Hunter Pack

To My Mother, Beatrice, thank you for always being my champion and installing in me the values of hard work, curiosity, and perseverance. I dedicate this book to you with all my heart. I am forever grateful to my husband, Rod, children, Phil and Tesha, and my granddaughter, Jas. They continue to push me beyond my limitations. My dear sister Loretta, thank you for being a solution-seeker and always being there for the family. I can't imagine this caregiving journey without you by my side. And Gail, thank you for inviting me to join the Wisdom Whisperers. I am thankful for being a part of this perceptive, caring sisterhood that shares wisdom through mindful storytelling.

E. Paulette Smith-Epps

I am indebted to my parents. They instilled a strong sense of self-worth, encouraged creativity, inspired me to love and appreciate life, and motivated me to strive for excellence rather than mediocrity. Even though they are no longer with us, their lessons remain in my heart and soul. I will always be grateful to them. Rosalyn Roberts Mack was my Group Leader of the Dogwoods. She has been diligent in keeping us on track and giving us pointers to help us refine our essays. Thank you, Gail Tusan Washington, for inviting me to participate and contribute to this publication. The experience has been cathartic and phenomenal. I thank my family for giving me space and time to write and create. Finally, I thank my late husband, William Given Epps, Sr., who afforded me a wonderful life and family. Without his life, my essay would not have been possible.

Gail Tusan Washington

In the final days of the creation of this book, I suffered a takotsubo cardiomyopathy episode. My life changed instantly, necessitating me to temporarily curtail my role as Convener/Lead Whisperer. Such was not an easy task. Our authors' collective means the world to me, and I did not want my own challenge to impede our journey together. I am deeply grateful to all the Wisdom Whisperers for their contributions to this collection of wisdom and their kindness extended to me during this scary, sobering personal time. But I am especially grateful to Rosalyn Mack, Beatrice Pack, and Joan Drescher for stepping in and their sacrifice of time to ensure our manuscript was completed timely. I especially wish to thank my mother, Lois Carrington Tusan, for her guidance every step of my 67-year journey. I am who I am because of who she is. Strong women raise strong women who raise strong women. My essay is dedicated to the four generations of Tusan/Washington women: my mom and stepmother, Margaret, daughters Ashley and Lauren, and granddaughter Kendall. You all inspire me and remind me of my value to our family. Yet, I must also thank my husband, Carl, for your unconditional support, sons, Shannon and Colin, and grandson, Cameron, for helping to ground me over the summer of 2023. Finally, Dad and Brian, never forget that you two are my heroes.

The Wisdom Whisperers

We greatly appreciate the editorial, creative, and technical assistance Monique Jewell Anderson and her talented team at Spirit Filled Creations, LLC, and Don Morgan Photography provided. Thanks also to Bensonetta Tipton Lane, one of our own, who provided invaluable tough love first-read editorial advice to each of us, her Sister Whisperers. We thank Imani Monica McCullough, @YANASisters, and Helen Mitchell, Founder of The Refresh Experience, Deeper than a Retreat, for helping us to connect and creatively tap into our inner wisdom during our Whisperers Retreat. They equipped us with inspirational words, practical advice for creating the personal space to be creative, and meditative tools for drawing on positive energy. Finally, the Wisdom Whisperers are grateful for you, our readers. You encouraged us to whisper some more. We listened and offer this special collection of stories to nourish your soul.

Loving Wisdom

A Second Collection of Stories That Nourish the Soul

Table of Contents

Introduction

"Be rich in wisdom, and you will be wealthy beyond measure."

Loving Wisdom, A Second Collection of Stories to Nourish the Soul, continues the gift that a group of eleven women gave in the first volume of Loving Wisdom three years ago. When we embarked on the journey that resulted in the publication of the first volume, none of us imagined that our collection of essays would have the impact that it had on its writers and readers. Particularly poignant was its birth and presentation as the world navigated the once-in-a-lifetime event of a pandemic. During this time of isolation and uncertainty, the nuggets of wisdom served as a source of inspiration to those who received it.

Similarly, the fifteen contributors to *Loving Wisdom, A Second Collection...*, have generously shared their stories of loss, trauma, triumph, resilience, tenacity, humility, learning, and love. The authors, Wisdom Whisperers, continue the storytelling tradition compellingly and insightfully. While conveying their experiences, the writers carefully transport the reader through the transformative power of their life-changing moments.

The reader first encounters Leslie Hazle Bussey's debut into poetry with her poignant prose, *What Would I Say.* She candidly shares her feelings as a parent of a transgender youth and allows us to feel her deep love for her precious child.

Triumph over trauma and loss is a theme in the stories of Rosalyn Roberts Mack, Lolita Browning Jackson, Roberta Jackson, Joyce Coleman Edwards, and E. Paulette Smith-Epps. These women openly expose the range of emotions and thoughts they experienced in these painful times and demonstrate the inner strength they possessed to carry them through the difficult times.

Gail Tusan Washington and Henrietta Stith Andrews engage the reader by sharing their stories of resilience, re-framing, and renewal, leading them to find, define, and live in their purpose despite naysayers and those who underestimate them. They show the power of being true to oneself and the riches that can be revealed when doing so.

Beatrice Hunter Pack and Malena Cunningham Anderson lovingly re-count their experiences with the difficult yet blessed task of caretaking. Being a caretaker of a loved one can be demanding and require all of the physical, emotional, and spiritual strength one can muster. As a caretaker, just as being a parent, one often wonders if you are doing the right thing. These writers are transparent and vulnerable in telling their stories. They nonetheless provide a view into the honor of supplying care.

Tisa Jackson allows us to learn about her journey with alopecia. For a woman in our society, hair is more than a part of one's physical being; it is often tied to how one is perceived and received in society. The reader is given a glimpse into the complex feelings evoked when a key part of one's appearance changes significantly.

In her essay, *The End*, Joan Wagnon Drescher addresses a topic many people are uncomfortable about approaching one's death. She enables the reader to learn what has caused her to reach her decision about how she wants to experience her "end."

La Verne C. Dixon shares how she reached a place of love, peace, and purpose as she navigates through her life's journey in her essay, *Grace and Mercy*.

Throughout these Loving Wisdom stories, certain common themes emerge. The writers discuss the importance of community, family, connections, and support. They also talk about the importance of listening to their *inner voice* in overcoming adversity and making hard decisions.

The Wisdom Whisperers' signature tree watermark is carried forward from their debut anthology, *Loving Wisdom,* and appears throughout these pages. The title of the watermark is *Autumn's First Fall* (24" x 24" framed) and was created by Henrietta Stith Andrews.

"Wisdom lives inside all who are quiet enough to listen to it."
~Anonymous

These essays are incredible in their beauty and depth, as are the women who have written them. Be awestruck by what they offer, be encouraged by the lessons they impart, and be inspired to share with others. Like love, wisdom is best when it is shared.

Nina R. Hickson

HOW
MEASURE UP?
54"

What I Would Say
By Leslie Hazle Bussey

Oh, my child.
If I could go back, I would choose empathy over fixing.
I wanted too many things when the only thing that mattered
was that you know that I see you. All of you.
And I love you.

Oh, my child.
If I could go back, I would say, "Tell me more."
I think I couldn't hear all of it. I wanted to "help" you
but I didn't create space to listen for what was beneath your words
so I could understand what help you needed.

Oh, my child.
If I could go back, I would say,
"That must feel so scary. You're not alone."
You needed me to see you, to sit with you, to hold you.
I didn't. It must have felt so lonely. So terrifying.
I can feel my heart pushing against my ribs as it tries to contain the
pain of thinking how you must have felt. How alone. How scared.
How angry.
And the pain of knowing I didn't show up for you.
Can you ever forgive me? Can I ever forgive myself?

Oh, my child.
If I could go back, I would say,
"There's nothing wrong with you. I am so proud of you."
There's nothing wrong with you. I am so proud of you.
Is it too late?
Can you possibly allow these words to flow into your heart
and offer a soothing salve of deep knowledge
that you aren't crazy? It wasn't you.

Words won't erase that you needed me, and I didn't (couldn't) give you what you needed.
But maybe these words can ease it.

Oh, my child.
If I could go back, I would say, "I'm sorry. I let you down. It's not your fault."
I can control my thoughts, my words, and my actions.
I can't make you hear or feel anything.
But I can fully own my pieces.
My heart never wakes without feeling this weight—this hole.
You will always have a home with me. You will always be my child.
You will always be a part of our family. And I have cultivated a space in my heart and spirit just for you that I hope you find is more curious and more generous.

Oh, my child.
We can't go back. But I can tell you
the only thing that matters and ever mattered
was that you know I see you. All of you.
And I love you.
The door is open. Come in and be loved how you
deserve to be loved.

Loss of a Loved One

"A great soul serves everyone all the time.

A great soul never dies.

It brings us together again and again."
~Maya Angelou, Author, Poet, and Civil Rights Activist

"The world changes from year to year,

Our lives from day to day,

but the love and memory of you shall

never pass away."
~Unknown

Christmas (Delaware) 1994

Oh, Happy Day!?
By Rosalyn Roberts Mack

I wondered the best way to share a life event that happened almost 30 years ago. I thought the circumstances would be etched in my heart and mind forever; however, miraculously, the years have dulled the pain and blurred the details. I wanted my recollection to be as accurate and authentic as possible, so I proceeded upstairs to the attic and searched through the many suitcases filled with journals from the last 45 years until I found the volumes that contained the years 1994 and 1995.

As I read the words, I was wowed. They took me instantly to a time of struggle and confusion as the strongminded woman in her 30s balanced a plethora of roles and was determined to execute them successfully. I read my journal entry, "...the year 1995 began with the usual blessings of family and friends but were quickly offset by the challenges of my career..." I cringed. I expended great effort to understand the politics of power and position as I observed organizational chaos resulting from ineffective leadership. Back then, I found the behavior I witnessed puzzling and disturbing. As I now know, power is not negative- it's what one chooses to do with it that inevitably advances humanity or diverts the path of progress. Reading further, the encounters seemed unnecessary- whether to accept a new position that I was being pressured to take or speak up to influence others to hear, understand, and consider my point of view. My carefully selected words, spoken with a mix of authority and deference, were like walking a verbal tightrope- sometimes getting more treacherous with each spoken word.

I smiled when I got to the parts about my joyous family life. My adoring husband and soulmate, Trentton, and I were blessed with a wonderful family. We had a beautiful daughter, Victoria, and were devoted to her and her well-being. As a two-career couple working in Corporate America, we successfully juggled our new life as parents with daycare, friends, family, faith, and all that involved being working parents. In addition to a myriad of other responsibilities, we had surprising news- I was pregnant *again*! After the initial shock and awe, we conducted another pregnancy test to be sure. *Positive!* My husband and I thanked God for the new life and prayed for its overall protection and purity of heart.

This is where my story of *Oh, Happy Day!?* began.

Pregnancy: The Journey

Trentton and I asked God to reveal His plan for this beautiful miracle growing inside me. Admittedly, I was not a spring chicken and recognized the need to do all I could to ensure my precious cargo, Baby Mack2, remained as healthy and happy as possible. So, I purged my diet per the doctor's orders- no caffeine, no alcohol, and began taking prenatal vitamins. I had a prophetic dream a few months prior, suggesting a baby boy would be joining our family. I thought, *Was this a coincidence, or had God sent me a message in a dream to help prepare me*? Trentton and I, though accepting and excited, were still in shock. We knew our lives would change significantly. As Trentton said, "...this is a real responsibility and will take planning, but let's admit this is truly God's will." Oh, Happy Day!?

In the following weeks, my pregnancy was uneventful, allowing me to continue demonstrating my commitment to my job in the male-dominated culture in which I worked. The months slipped by quickly as I continued to modify my wardrobe to conceal my ever-expanding physique. My chic, albeit loose-fitting, wardrobe did an excellent job of disguising and hiding my baby bump. Though I don't think it was called that back in 1995, times have truly changed. Women today proudly show their baby bumps and do not try to hide them under those horrid tent dresses. I am so impressed - that's a measure of progress. I did not wear tent dresses but rather soft flowing outfits with blazers. My professional persona dictated that I remain business-like, so boxy blazers (with shoulder pads) were my cover-up, and they worked well for me.

However, when I started to protrude noticeably, I thought about when and how to inform my manager and team that a bun was in the oven. But back then, pregnancy could be viewed as a reason to limit a woman's upward mobility, relegating her to the infamous *mommy track*. My reveal needed to be strategically and carefully orchestrated. In today's corporate world, sharing such news is not a big deal – often resulting in elaborate and festive reveal parties.

When Spring approached, our business group hosted a picnic, and we were required to RSVP. Doing so would be cute and funny for 3.5 people- Trentton, Victoria, me, and Baby Mack2. Yes, co-workers found it comical, and the news (i.e., gossip) of my pregnancy spread like wildfire. My colleagues wanted to know if I would continue to work after the birth. I suspected they secretly hoped I would stay home to reduce the number of viable candidates for upcoming promotions, but I told them, "My husband and I are committed to balancing work and family in a way that supports our family and both of our careers." I imagined hearing them say, "Darn!" But we all continued to conduct business as usual, except I reduced and soon eliminated any air travel- to minimize all risks and to ensure Baby Mack2's future.

As the warmer weather arrived, I planted beautiful flowers in our garden to enjoy once the baby arrived. No heavy lifting was required, just selecting and planting flowers of my choosing. Just like we did with Victoria, Trentton and I communicated with Baby Mack2 daily by tapping on my tummy. Communication, after all, is about transmitting a message and receiving a response. We were certain our private Morse code delivered loving messages because we received the soft and loving responding kicks. Time passed slowly as the heaven-sent tap and kick rhythm captivated us and brought smiles to our faces.

My journal entries continued to describe work events: meetings, product launches, profit margins, target retailers, etc. Business proceeded as usual- nothing out of the ordinary, then the journal entries stopped. The pages were blank, no words, no markings whatsoever. I'm reminded of the day when we went silent - no words, no markings- our world changed forever.

The Day Our World Stood Still

I enlisted Trentton to help fill the gaps, and we were hopeful that, together, our memories would provide the tools needed to accurately excavate the events of the days missing from the 28-year-old journal. Over a few adult beverages and dinner, the rain fell, and we were struck by the symbolism of the tears that were shed. We easily peeled back one layer at a time of the eerie events. As we exchanged our recollections, it became clear that *the day* had remained etched in our minds and souls, and we relived them together again.

Wednesday, May 24, 1995, appeared to be an ordinary sunny mild-weathered day. Trentton proceeded to work and planned to meet me at the doctor's office for our appointment. I had come to expect bodily changes with pregnancy, so the slight physical discomfort I felt didn't concern either of us. After he arrived, we were assigned an exam room and were joined by one of our favorite nurses. She chatted away, outgoing and chipper as usual, and recorded my results. All my vitals were a-okay.

Next, the tech came in focused and ready to proceed with the examination. She began inquiring about my discomfort as she prepared me for an ultrasound. I described my heaviness to her, which differed from prior days, even though I was convinced it was nothing. As I did, I noticed she suddenly stopped and applied another glob of gel to my tummy. Her all-about-business demeanor didn't alarm me because she had always been that way, and her expression didn't show concern as she left the room. Trentton and I resumed our conversation while we waited for the doctor to come in.

A knock interrupted our conversation, and the door slowly opened. We were surprised to see another tech enter, along with the first. She repeated the ultrasound procedure. After a long look at the screen, and before both techs left, they casually mentioned that my OB/GYN, Dr. Whitney, would be with us shortly. Trentton and I remained jovial and unphased as we awaited her arrival.

Dr. Whitney, a petite woman with a strong physique, wore neat and eloquent braids, which showed off her sense of pride. I had always admired her for these qualities and her thoroughness and honesty. During our professional relationship, Trentton and I gained complete confidence in her. After the usual greetings, she, too, repeated the ultrasound. She looked at the monitor for what seemed like hours, though only minutes passed by, and then, with sadness in her eyes and an uncharacteristically quivering voice, she informed us that Baby Mack2 wasn't moving – the heart that normally pulsed with life lay still. I respectfully told her I felt the baby moving as she spoke. She then explained that in the amniotic fluid, it might appear the baby was moving, even kicking, but that was not the case.

Our world froze. Our brains could not comprehend her words; they sounded foreign as if she spoke a language we neither knew nor understood. Trentton and I looked at each other silently- we needed more clarity. What did she mean? Was this like our first child who was so anxious to enter the world that I went into premature labor, resulting in mandatory bedrest to help slow things down? We could deal with that, but what did *no heartbeat* mean? We came to understand that BabyMack2 had died.

Trentton and I sobbed endlessly as the nurses tried to comfort us. Instinctively, we held on to one another – hugging, caressing, and trying to console the other. We were given lots of time to gather our thoughts in the exam room. We were devastated, which is an understatement - staring into space - not understanding why the universe dealt us this catastrophic blow. We felt like zombies, stuck and abandoned on one of life's roads we didn't choose. We were powerless.

Dr. Whitney returned and informed us that she had scheduled a date and time to induce labor to deliver the baby. My mind searched for understanding as I tried to clearly comprehend her words. "I have to give birth to a baby whose heart has stopped beating?" I asked.

"Yes," Dr. Whitney said with soft compassion.

"And the scheduled date is two days from now?"

"Yes," she said, then warned us we may see tissue loss from the baby's decomposing body. Trentton and I were emotionally paralyzed and could only rely on Dr. Whitney's care and delivery options expertise.

Trentton and I didn't do much for the next two days as we awaited the ill-fated delivery procedure. When I moved, I felt Baby Mack2 move also- it reminded me of the baby kicks that brought us such joy just a week ago. *Could there be a mistake? Could Baby Mack2 miraculously regain its health?* I pondered. We were both in denial as we dug deep inside to hang on – that's all we had: each other, our faith, and hope.

The day of, I told Dr. Whitney I felt the baby move and insisted on another ultrasound before anything commenced. I observed the slight glances between the medical staff, but they graciously abided by my wishes. They turned the monitor towards me and showed me Baby Mack2's motionless body. Trentton and I had no choice but to accept the stark reality that there were no more taps, kicks, or morse-code moments because Baby Mack2's soul had transitioned to life everlasting before her physical body left my womb.

With deep sadness, the process of medically inducing labor began. The contractions were strong – I pushed – the familiar pulsating pain reminded me of the delivery of Victoria. However, I knew this was vastly different – this delivery would culminate with BabyMack2's lifeless body exiting my body. At 7:05 pm, the medical staff sorrowfully watched Trentton witness the umbilical cord tightly wrapped around BabyMack2's little neck. The face plagued with anguish- we could only imagine the tragic struggle for life in my womb. After gaining his composure, Trentton announced as only a proud father could, "It's a beautiful baby girl!" And we wept.

The hospital arranged a grief counselor who advised us to name her, hold her, talk to her, take pictures with her, and pray with her. We were both traumatized by the experience of giving birth to a lifeless body, but we heeded the grief counselor's advice and named her Tiffany Ann Mack. After Tiffany Ann had been cleaned and wrapped in a lovely white blanket, we were given precious time to honor her in our special way. As I held her close, with her arms neatly folded across her body, I studied her face. I, too, saw her anguish.

The sterile and quiet room contributed to the somber mood, so we did the only thing we knew to do at that moment: pray. Afterward, the hospital clergy came and baptized her, and the nurses gently carried her away, and we were left to decide how to proceed next- cremation or burial. Trentton and I had never discussed our burial preferences or post-life beliefs (we never needed to), but we needed to decide. Eventually, after a heart-wrenching discussion, we decided to bury her.

This once joyful married couple was grief-stricken beyond words. We left the hospital holding tightly to each other as we walked into the warm night air. We silently slipped into our car and drove home. The next day, we informed Victoria, our two-year-old, that her little sister wore angelic wings and resided in heaven. Victoria was amazing. She exhibited love, concern for us, and care. She did not cry nor show signs of confusion or worry. She most likely didn't understand the concept of dying and loss, but her bravery and engaging personality helped ground us at such a highly emotional time.

We were in a task-focused mode, which allowed us to get through the macabre job of burying our brand-new baby. After heart-wrenching but thoughtful consideration, we chose to have Tiffany Ann's burial at Trentton's family's beautiful plot in Connecticut. We found comfort in knowing Tiffany Ann's small body would lay buried among her ancestors who, we imagined, had warmly welcomed her upon arrival in heaven. In her tiny casket, we placed a letter that read:

To Our Dear Sweet Tiffany Ann:

What a brief time our time together has been. The day we discovered you were with us...yes, we were shocked...but we were so delighted. It seemed almost mystical that you entered our lives at that time. We still have your very first sonogram picture. It went everywhere we went. And the subsequent pictures were wonderful, too! You lay in my belly so majestically.

As we considered names, we wanted your first name to begin with a 'T' to follow the Mack tradition. Tiffany seemed so perfect for you. We had just purchased a Tiffany lamp that was so delicate, intricate, and beautiful. The beauty is breathtaking when the light shines through the colored glass. That is how we imagined you! A beautiful spirit, especially when your 'light' was shining (which we know would always be). The name 'Ann' is for your Grandmother Roberts, a strong and beautiful Black woman. Tiffany Ann, Tiffany Ann – what a beautiful name for a beautiful spirit.

We saw you and held you after your delivery. Your face was precious. We sensed struggle in your face, though. I hope your experience in the womb wasn't too traumatic.

We trust you're in a good place now. We have been praying for you continuously. Should you ever want to come this way again, we'll be honored to have you come through us again. Until then, may the Lord Bless You and Keep You. May He Lift His Face to Shine Upon You and Give You Peace.

We Love You with All our Hearts and Soul!
Your Parents and Sister

A Sweet Goodbye

The bright sun lingered in the blue sky while the mild, crisp air caressed my skin. I always loved the elegance of the 270 acres of rolling hills that comprise Cedar Hill Cemetery in Hartford, CT. I'd been there many times to honor the grave of Trentton's dad, but I never imagined I would need to utilize the stately plot for my child. The graveside service, though formal, captured the spirit and sweet simplicity of our dear departed daughter. Our family and friends sent beautiful flowers and other expressions of love to support us. In attendance were my parents, Trentton's mom, and, of course, Victoria.

My deep and heavy sorrow rested in the depths of my heart until Victoria's sweet and carefree spirit lifted it. She tended to Tiffany Ann's gravesite like an adoring older sister would. She hovered over the site, appearing like she didn't want to leave her. We took pictures of Victoria at the gravesite to always remember that moment – Victoria's purity of heart coupled with our faith. The day is still etched in my memory.

After the funeral, we returned to Delaware, where I paced the floors of the house, trying to collect my thoughts. Devastated, I wondered how best to deal with my grief. Did I need the counseling the hospital graciously offered me after my delivery? Or maybe a support group would be better? Trentton and I decided to work through our feelings ourselves, without outside influence or assistance – we would lean on our faith and each other- and we did. It took time, but life got brighter and easier with each day. I began responding to the numerous cards, letters, gifts, and acts of kindness we received.

I was touched by the number of co-workers who rallied by my side with heartfelt messages and kind words. Some shared stories of their losses from troubled pregnancies. They shared their hope and faith and encouraged me to cling to mine. As I continued to crawl out from under my despair, I thought about what lessons I could take away from this experience, so I started writing.

Epilogue: The Unexpected Gifts

I resumed my journal entries after Tiffany Ann's funeral service. I began writing to force myself to shift perspectives. Our experience rocked us to our core, *but* if Tiffany Ann's short life with us on earth was meant to reveal blessings, what could they be? This thought process jolted my mind in an attempt to pull myself out of a seemingly bottomless pit of pity and grief. I once heard, "If you can't change your circumstances, change how you think about them." In an attempt to do that, I noted the blessings of Tiffany Ann's short life, which included:

- She reinforced my belief system. I had endured the loss of Tiffany Ann's physical body, but her spirit lived in the hearts of many. I remembered that God stood with me and promised never to leave nor forsake me.

- She reminded me of the love of family and friends, who rallied around us in our time of greatest need.

- Her short life emphasized the need to hold life dear and to live it with a joyous heart.

- My love and grief for her are authentic and valued feelings, and I should never be ashamed to demonstrate them.

- Acceptance: I learned to accept things, people, and situations. Having faith that everything is happening at the divine right time and God is ordering my steps.

- She reinforced my principle of not judging others: Knowing what people have been through is difficult and nearly impossible. We can't know the entirety of each other's story, but everyone has a story.

With this huge hole in my heart, I forged on and committed to something good coming from knowing, loving, and ultimately losing Tiffany Ann. We received her death certificate approximately three weeks following her birth, and it set us back, but we had the faith and fortitude to continue moving forward, which was a good place to be. And with God's grace, the years passed, and as they did, life got easier. A few years later, we were blessed with a wonderful son, Joshua, and the months, years, and decades continue to fly by- one joyous moment after another.

Lolita With Her Father

Credibility: A Story of Loss, Healing, and Connecting
By Lolita Browning Jackson

Reality Used To Be My Friend

The day was February 5, 1978. I was a happy-go-lucky eight-year-old girl who loved playing with her dolls, jumping rope, and riding her bike in the neighborhood with friends. I remember running into the house that Sunday morning after being away the night before at a sleepover at my friend Ree Ree's house. Ree Ree, whose actual name is Aurelia, and I were the best of friends. Our parents were good friends also, so we were at each other's homes all the time. Her mother dropped me off, and upon running inside the house, I saw my dad lying on the living room couch. I gave him a big hello hug and asked where everyone was. He shared that my sisters were upstairs, and the others were at church with my mother. I excitedly ran upstairs to see what my big sisters were doing. As a little sister of five older siblings, all teenagers, I was interested in their teen life shenanigans. They would say I was being nosey.

I don't recall the conversations with my sisters or even what they were doing, but I followed my sister, Belinda, downstairs, and the next thing I saw was a commotion in the living room. She had called the emergency number, and paramedics were in our home, taking my father out on a stretcher. My mother and other siblings were now home from church and were standing by my father's side. I thought it was odd that there was a fire truck outside, not an ambulance; that's when I learned that firefighters were emergency medical technicians and first responders. Still, I was somewhat confused because when I hugged Daddy, he seemed fine to me. He was his loving, affectionate self as I put my face to his cheek. I can still feel how the hair stubble was tickly against my skin.

My father had a stroke, and I didn't know how bad it was. I vaguely recall family coming into town to visit. That may have been a sign that he was not doing well. Back then, children were not allowed to visit the hospital except on Sundays. So, I was excited and looking forward to that day because my younger sister, Sylvia, and I would get to see him. It was a long week as I waited for Sunday to arrive. Finally, the Lord's Day came. I sat on the steps that morning after breakfast, watching as my mother answered the telephone attached to the kitchen wall. It was the doctor. They wanted her to get to the hospital right away. I could tell it was bad because of my mother's sad, quiet tone. I immediately learned we could not go with her. We would never see our father, Q.V. Browning, alive again. The last day I saw Daddy alive was February 5; he passed away on February 12, 1978. Both dates are etched in my memory forever. Years later, in 2018, on February 5, my older sister, Cindy, passed away. I don't believe in coincidences. I believe in divine order. My father was waiting for her as she passed. I was so devastated when my father died, and I didn't know how to express my feelings, let alone process them all. And so, I cried to myself. I dreamed of flying in the sky like an angel. I pretended my father was reincarnated in birds or another life. I envisioned him coming back. During this time, my mother taught me to pray, which I did every night before bed and in the mornings when I awakened. I simply learned to talk to God whenever I thought I needed to. I have done so every day since.

Shortly after my father passed, everyone began preparing for his funeral services. My mother was so strong. She was a skilled seamstress and made Sylvia's and my dresses for the services. I believe sewing was therapy for her and her being resourceful. There was a service in Waukegan, Illinois, a suburb of Chicago where we lived. We then went to another service in my mother's hometown, Brownsville, Tennessee, where she ultimately buried him in a family cemetery near her father, who had passed away five years earlier.

Soon, family encouraged my mother to move to Brownsville, Tennessee. There, she would be closer to her mother and other relatives. We also would be a little closer to Camden, Arkansas, my father's hometown, where his oldest sister, Aunt Willie B, lived. Also, New Orleans, Louisiana, was near where our favorite Aunt, our father's older sister Vivian, lived. She resided in Chicago and visited with us regularly throughout our childhood. She moved after my father passed away. So, Mommy, let us finish the school year that spring. We had a wonderful summer in Waukegan with friends and summer camps while she had the house painted and prepped for sale. With the move to Brownsville, the dynamics of my life, my friends, and my home would forever change. I believe my father's death defined who I would grow to be and how I would approach life. The good thing about Brownsville was learning about my family roots on my mom's side. My maternal grandmother was close by, and we were able to build a good, loving relationship with her. Additionally, my older siblings went to colleges nearby. So, the younger four of us grew up in Brownsville. Yet, I would miss our home in Waukegan. It held my memories with my father. I etched every inch of that house in my mind to retain everything I could about him; who he was, his friendships, his personality, and his voice. Remembering became important to me and remains a strong part of who I am today. My friends often say, "You have a great memory." Now, I know why. I intentionally stored away specifics about my father, our life together, and what he taught me. It was my way of respecting him. I learned the basic skills needed to function. He taught me to tie my shoes when I went to kindergarten and even how to put a worm on a fishing rod for him when he went fishing. He taught me not to be afraid of dogs, to be okay with not following what friends may do, and to be my own person. I cherish all I learned from him. Today, remembering is my way of showing people I'm listening to them, I care about what is being said, and I'll remember. Studies show a child's most formative years are from birth to eight. So, by the time my father passed, I had learned a great deal from him and my mother.

That summer, we loaded all our belongings into a huge U-Haul with our station wagon hitched to the back, and we left what I knew as home and moved *down south*, as my siblings and friends would say. Although we were in a new place, my mother and other family were sure to help us remember Q.V. Browning. The stories shared about him over the years were never-ending. In Brownsville, our mother, a preschool educator, opened and ran a child development center. She was an expert at teaching three and four-year-old children how to read and write. Interestingly, her daycare center sat across the street from the family cemetery where our father was buried. When she moved home, she brought him with her. We grew up visiting the cemetery regularly. We took flowers on holidays, like Father's Day and Memorial Day. I would talk to him through the dirt like he was there. Growing up without my father was not my reality. It was as if he was always with us but not really with us. Because of this, I never really thought of my mother as a single mother. In my mind, I had a father there. Who he was and how he parented was prevalent through conversations with us growing up. She was a single parent, a fact I didn't truly get until I was grown and gone from home. As I watched my mother, I learned that I wasn't the only one sad, and I prayed for her. I prayed for my siblings, aunts and uncles, his friends, and everyone I thought would miss him as I did. And because my mother taught me how to pray, God's healing, blessings, and love came with it. Over the years, our mother went out of her way to ensure we had a full life. With my five older siblings away in college, I was proud to be the oldest at home. My mother shared with me what this meant. It meant being a leader, taking responsibility, and loving each other. I took this role seriously. She taught us to love and support each other no matter what.

There is a saying that everything in life happens for a reason. Learning to live without my father made me resilient and taught me to be intentional about relationships. I often wonder if I would have grown to be as strong had he not passed when I was so young. Living without him also taught me to value connections. I believe deeply in authentic, genuine connections. I'm compassionate about the bonds of friendship and family. Learning to cope with his death also made me compassionate. Having to leave a home I knew, move to a new town, attend a new school, and make new friends was a bit challenging for the quiet, shy little girl I was. However, I did it.

Connecting to people became important to me and remains so today. As a child, I learned it was up to me to be happy. Making life work for me as a little girl in a new home, new town, and new school was my first lesson in choosing happiness. I believe learning to accept his death prepared me for the many next steps I would take in life as I grew and matured.

After graduating from college in Tennessee, I moved to Atlanta, Georgia, where three of my older siblings lived. I was blessed to land a job in my field as a print news reporter, fulfilling my dream to become a journalist. But navigating the transition into adulthood was particularly challenging for me, mentally. I had been out of college for three years and worked as a newspaper writer and reporter. I was good at it, winning awards, doing investigative pieces, and interviewing politicians, celebrities, and well-known leaders. However, I moved through the motions of life, feeling sad and lonely. Special moments would make me feel sad as I often wished I had my father with me to celebrate. Celebratory moments such as graduating from college, getting my first front-page news story, and starting a new job were all sad for me. Many of the new friends and colleagues I met along the way would learn immediately upon connecting with me that my father had passed. While it had been many years since he died, I treated and expressed it as if it were just yesterday. I would often get an instant response from someone expressing their condolences or sympathy as they believed it had happened recently based on how I shared my sadness. I shared that my father had actually passed when I was eight years old with a new friend one day, and the response shattered me on the inside when the person said, "That was so long ago, you probably don't remember him." It was so nonchalant and matter-of-fact that it felt like someone had kicked me in my stomach, leaving me feeling crushed, broken, and not credible.

It was then, at 24 years old, when it came closing in on me. Not having my father left me feeling lonely. In my loneliness, I thought life would be better if I was not here. If I was to die, I'd be closer to my father. If I just died, I'd be able to see and live with him again- in Heaven. I had lived many moments thinking my life was not credible without my father. Especially when I saw other girls with theirs, I felt that not having his presence left me unworthy. I strived for my degree, an awesome career, and journalism awards, thinking these things would create a level of worthiness I didn't feel. After an attempted suicide, I spent some needed time with my father's youngest sister, Aunt Jean, in Colorado, along with Uncle Kemp and my cousins. Over the years, we had grown close; she was the closest of my father's siblings to his age. She would share the stories of what he was like as a teenager when they were in high school. I loved hearing those stories. The visit was good for me. Being with them and hearing stories about my daddy helped me to feel even closer to him. When someone close to you dies, you never get over it; you learn to live without them. Having lost my father at such a young age and not having gone to therapy at that time, I lived for years to come in constant yearning for him. By the time I was 24, the grief overwhelmed me as I had not yet emotionally learned to live without him.

After my respite in Colorado, I returned to Atlanta, and Belinda suggested I see a psychiatrist. She took me to the first visit, which was very beneficial, as he helped me to see that I had never truly mourned the loss of my father as a child. The therapist helped me see that I was destroying my happiness and making myself sad in happy moments, such as when I graduated from college or received an award. I was encouraged to write a letter to Daddy saying goodbye. I laid it all out, sharing those happy moments he missed with me, and then I said, "Goodbye."

I had to move on. I had to let him go and let go of the eight-year-old little girl inside of me. Through ongoing therapy, journaling, and prayer, I worked on myself. During those days, nearly 30 years ago, I learned how to move forward and not backward. I joined a new church, built new friendships, and flourished in my career, eventually returning to school to get a Master of Business Administration in Marketing. I built the confidence to live for myself. I began to understand that I did have a father, and his dying did not make me less creditable or less worthy of anything life had to offer. I worked through my depression and focused on my career. I am blessed with a large, loving, caring family and loyal and devoted friends. In time, I realized that I could create a new, more friendly reality for myself to live fully. And while God has a plan for me, it was up to me to choose to listen and follow his guidance to receive the many blessings He has for me. Being a better Lolita helped me be a better daughter, sister, aunt, friend, and ultimately a wife and mother. I truly believe the work I put in to love myself, being prayerful, faithful, and fearless, led me to attract the love of my life, John Michael Jackson. Knowing that my father would approve of him brings me great joy, satisfaction, and peace. Knowing my connection to my father, my oldest sister, Elma Jean, ensured he was with me as I walked down the aisle on my wedding day. She embroidered my favorite picture of my father and me into the pillow the ring bearer carried down the aisle. During the ceremony, my sisters lit a candle in memory of Daddy. My self-care, therapy, journaling, exercising, and praying also prepared me to be a dynamic mother to our son, Aaron, who is now 16. I have shared with my son who my father was, and he has a photo of him playing football in his room. He knows the roots from which he comes.

While my father's death taught me the meaning of loss at an early age, his death also taught me the value and significance of connection. Connecting with people and building professional and personal relationships has been an important part of my life.

I know now that my father is always in my life as he lives in me, in my heart. His love was so strong that I carry all I learned from him in eight short years with me every day. I now live each day, fully appreciating life and all it brings.

The smiles of a little girl and her daddy!

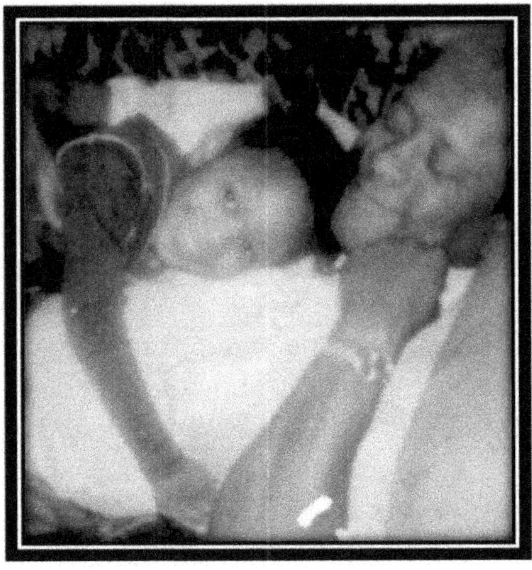

THE END

Loving Wisdom
A Second Collection of Stories That Nourish the Soul

1989
By Joyce Coleman Edwards

If ever there was a year in my life I would erase, it would be 1989. It started rocky and got worse. In January, a woman who was my live-in nanny died. I wasn't informed of her death until a month later. This was a tragedy for me because I could not attend the funeral. It would have meant the world for me to have been able to tell her goodbye because our relationship meant so much. She was like a grandmother to me. In April, my father-in-law, whom I had grown close to since he moved from Chicago to Atlanta, was killed when trying to help a stranded woman on the highway and was hit by several cars as he crossed over to assist her.

In May, my divorce from my first husband was finalized. We had been married for seven years when we decided to part ways. I didn't realize how stressful going through a divorce could be. We separated for two years until the divorce was final. I thought that life would go on and I would slowly adjust to making a life for me and my 6-year-old son Jonathan. What I hadn't anticipated was that I would grieve the death of my marriage just as if a loved one had died.

At the end of June, my ex-husband took our son to Chicago for the July 4th holiday. I was to go along but had a scheduling conflict. Nevertheless, I was glad Jonathan could go because he could see my parents, my husband's parents, and most of his relatives. The visit went fine, and they had a wonderful time. My son lost his two front teeth while on this trip, and I was anxious to see his toothless grin. They were due to return home on July 5. They left my mother-in-law's house around 1 p.m. and headed south to Atlanta.

I was called shortly afterward but was only told there had been an accident. I was called by the hospital chaplain, who informed me that my son was no longer alive. A fast-moving cement truck struck and drove over their car. A crane had to lift the truck off. The *jaws of life* were used to pry open the top of my ex's car to get him and our son out. When they got the top opened, what was seen was a testament to what kind of man and father he was; he was on top of Jonathan. He tried to save his son's life with his own. I didn't know until several hours later they had both reached the hospital dead on arrival.

That's when my world stopped turning!

I was devastated by the news and went through the necessary rituals of informing relatives and preparing for his service while my heart broke into a million pieces. The next few days passed at a whirlwind pace. I had to pack a bag and make plane reservations for Chicago. Thank goodness one of my close friends was a travel agent. She got me a ticket to leave the next morning. Her sister flew to Atlanta to meet me and accompanied me so I wouldn't be on the plane alone. I stayed at my parent's home once I got there. I'm an only child, and we were very close. I don't know how I would have made it through without them. Making funeral arrangements, writing an obituary, and picking out his clothes kept me busy but were heartbreaking tasks. I didn't know how to write an obit for a six-year-old. I managed to finish it, but as I reflect, I was in such a daze, just going through the motions, trying to make it through minute by minute. I would wake up in the mornings feeling like I had a physical weight on my chest. I felt like I couldn't catch my breath. My mom would talk to me and make me feel better. As I learned, many more days like that would come.

The following Sunday in Chicago, we had their funeral at my mother-in-law's family church. Over 1,200 people came to the wake and service. My ex-husband was buried in Chicago. I chose to bring my son back to Atlanta, where we had an added funeral and burial service. Ironically, I didn't realize I had scheduled his Atlanta services on my birthday. I *buried* my son on my birthday. I couldn't believe it! It had totally slipped my mind. It was too late to change, so we had to proceed as scheduled. After the funeral, it took me days to get a good night's sleep. Two of my best friends came over one night to keep me company. As time passed and it became quite late, I wondered when they would go home. Little did I know they were thinking when I would get sleepy, too, so they could leave. Finally, around 2 a.m., we all started yawning and laughing at each other. This was one of the many times I had to laugh to keep from crying.

After my son's death, I not only saw everything differently, but I was a different person. There was a hole in my heart that would never close. He was rarely out of my thoughts. My parents and friends were wonderful; I would have never survived the process without them. They were very understanding in trying to help me put my life back together. In life, we are trained in many areas, but when it comes to grieving the loss of a loved one, especially a child, there is just no preparation for it. It just doesn't seem natural. Children should die after their parents. That is the natural order of life.

Grief is not something we are taught to deal with. The grieving process is real, and going through it is painful. There are five steps to it: denial, anger, bargaining, depression, and finally, acceptance. I went through every one of them. And not always in that order. There were days when I was angry at God for taking my son away. On other days, I would be depressed because I let him go to Chicago with his dad. If I had made a different decision, he would still be here. But that didn't make sense because why wouldn't I let him go with his dad to visit family and friends? There were also days when I felt guilty because I hadn't thought about him that day. Did that mean I didn't care or didn't love him? So many crazy emotions rushed over me while I was grieving the loss of my child. What helped me get through the process was an organization called Compassionate Friends. It is a support group for parents who have lost children. Fifty years ago, a chaplain at a hospital in England put two families together who had just suffered the loss of a child. He noticed that they offered each other comfort and hope that clergy or medical professionals couldn't because they hadn't had the experience of this kind of loss. I attended for several months, learning how to cope, gaining much insight into the process, and listening to other parents dealing with their grief. I learned that men and women grieve differently. Society allows women to grieve longer than men. Men are expected to suffer for a certain period, then get over it and move on. Women can grieve much longer and aren't criticized for taking as much time as needed. When I greet a couple who has suffered such a loss, I always go to the man first, letting him know that it's okay to take as much time as needed to learn to deal with a *new normal* of life.

In the months after Jonathan's death, I went through the motions of trying to have a life, but it did not work.

When you suffer a traumatic situation, your brain checks out, and your emotions take over. The problem with that concept is that your brain can think. Your emotions have the capacity to feel. Your brain cannot feel, and your emotions can't think. So, when your brain says, "I can't handle this situation," it checks out and leaves your emotions to think for you. Most decisions require thinking to make sense and flush out the details. Thinking with your feelings skips those steps, and you can make bad decisions.

Luckily, I didn't make too many, but my life was a mess, and even though I thought I was doing okay, I was not, and it was beginning to show up in the quality of work I was producing or not producing. I was an administrative assistant, forgetting things I should have been doing and making mistakes on work I had done for years. My emotions were all over the place. At home, I was having trouble sleeping and coping with a very empty home. Living in my apartment without Jonathan was, at times, unbearable. I would visit his gravesite often just to be close to him.

Six months after the accident, I quit my job. I had been in the Air Force as a reservist for many years, so I took the opportunity to take a five-week leadership course. I had to get away from anything that required thinking or using my brain. It was good to just get away and not have to think. In my new capacity as a leadership student, I could attend class and mechanically and mindlessly do what I was told. I had to make that break to get focused again. After I completed my course, I stayed on active duty. I thought it would be until 1990, but Desert Shield/Storm happened. I ended up staying on active duty for 2 ½ years. It was the best thing that I could have done for myself. It gave me time to heal and at least get a grip on myself and how I was feeling and coping with such a tremendous loss. After I left active duty, I returned to the job I left after the accident.

Mentally recovering from a very traumatic experience is more than a notion. At least if it were a physical injury, it would heal over time, and the scar would fade after a while. I have lived with this loss for over 35 years. I'm not going to say that I'll ever get over it, but I have recovered a *quality of life* that has given me the strength to get past it and survive the trauma. That doesn't mean I don't think about him often or don't have my moments when I find myself bawling like a baby as if it happened yesterday. Every year, between June 5, his birthday, and July 5, the day of his death, I mourn his loss more than any time of the year. Then there's Christmas, Mother's Day, graduations, and other events reminding me he's not here with me. I know I'll always be affected by his loss, but I don't allow it to define me.

"Life is like a box of chocolates; you never know what you are going to get," is a quote from the movie *Forrest Gump*. As outlined, my life has certainly been that way. Ups, downs, highs, and lows have all had their place in my humble existence. My life was on an even keel until 1989 when a series of unforeseeable tragedies ripped me from my foundation. My upbringing and faith helped me weather storms and hard times when I thought I would never survive. My experiences could have killed me, but they did not. They certainly changed the whole trajectory of my life. They stopped me in my tracks, flipped me upside down, slammed me against the wall, and blew up my whole world. I survived through God's twins, Grace and Mercy, and found my *new normal*. I have returned to a life of happiness and hope that I thought I would never achieve.

I married again, gained children and grandchildren, and my life has been enriched by moving on. I've counseled and supported other parents who have lost children. I try to show them a light at the end of the tunnel. I was lucky to have my faith, family, and friends who supported me throughout. I am, however, a living witness. A great loss can be overcome.

When you are going through something like this, it's good to connect with someone who has gone through the same thing. You can regain a quality of life even when you think you will never have peace again. Losing a child is the most tragic thing to happen to a parent. You can LIVE again. It takes time, and you must put the work in. It's not always easy, but when you come out of it and the sun shines again, the memories will bring you much joy and happiness!

Have You Ever Loved Someone

By E. Paulette Smith-Epps

A poem dedicated to William Given Epps, Sr.

Have you ever loved someone so much that you wondered how you lived before you met them?

Have you ever loved someone so much that when the person entered the room, your heart skipped a beat, and your pulse rate escalated?

Have you ever loved someone so much that the thought of being away from them made you wonder how you were going to continue living until you could see them again?

Have you ever loved someone so much that your heart actually ached when you knew they were emotionally distraught, discouraged, or disappointed with the vicissitudes of life?

Have you ever loved someone so much that being in their presence meant that all was right in the world and that joy and happiness were guaranteed?

Have you ever loved someone so much that you thought your heart would break in two at the sight of them ill, and there was nothing you could do to help them recover?

Have you ever loved someone so much that you prayed that you would die before them so that you would not have to suffer their loss?

Have you ever? Have you ever? Have you ever?

June 2009

On Becoming a Widow
By E. Paulette Smith-Epps

The Beginning

On March 15, 2017, at five o'clock in the morning, my life changed forever! My husband, William (Bill) Given Epps, Sr., was lying beside me and would not wake up. He was sleeping and breathing but would not wake up. I made the 9-1-1 call. While waiting for medical help, I called our children, who came immediately. Within minutes of my call, the Fire Department treated my beloved Bill in my bedroom.

The trip to the Emergency Room was difficult because we were at the beginning of rush-hour traffic in Atlanta. It felt like it took forever to finally get to the hospital. Unfortunately, there was no hospital in my neighborhood. We had to go to downtown Atlanta to get the medical help Bill needed. I should have known that there would not be a good outcome because my family was ushered into a private waiting room. By this time, two of my three children, three grandchildren, and Godson were waiting with me. Our oldest son, who lives in Michigan, was on the telephone. Thank God that my family surrounded me. It seemed like an eternity as we waited to hear from the doctor. It took hours.

While we waited, we started calling family, priests, and friends. These calls were so difficult to make because we had no details of a diagnosis and prognosis. All we could do was ask for prayer until we heard from the medical professionals. I felt hopeful and prayed that Bill's condition would improve.

Finally, the doctor came into our room and delivered the horrible news. My Bill had had a significant brain bleed, and nothing could be done to repair or fix the situation. We were devastated. Bill was still in an emergency treatment room. I went in to see him. As I lovingly caressed him, I noticed he still had on his jewelry. I was instructed to remove it, and I did so. Each piece flooded me with a lifetime of emotions because I knew he would never wear his cherished jewelry again."

His wedding band was first. He received it from me on our wedding day, May 5, 1979. It was a custom-made, wide band with herringbone texture engraved with our initials and wedding date. Bill and I were married in Atlanta, Georgia, at Union Baptist Church. It was a very hot and beautiful day. There were nearly 400 people present.

Next, I tenderly removed his gold cross pendant. I had purchased it in Chicago five years before ever meeting Bill or knowing he would become my husband. When I purchased it, I knew I would never wear it. I had it gift-wrapped in anticipation that someday I would meet my soul mate, and it would be a perfect symbol of our love. Years later, Bill unwrapped the gift on our wedding altar and wore it lovingly until that day at the hospital.

Third was a gold Figaro bracelet that was always on his right wrist. I gave it to Bill for our first Christmas together. It felt like I was preparing his body for his death. As I removed each piece, I was removing a part of myself. I cried silently as burning tears rolled down my cheeks, met under my chin, and dropped onto the bed sheets. My heart was pounding. My heart actually ached.

Reluctantly, I left Bill and went back to the room with the family as they took Bill to the ICU. We were taken to another private waiting room there. A hospital representative came and discussed hospice care. I could not hear the word *hospice*. No, not now. Just a few hours ago, I had been sleeping in bed with my husband. How did we transition to hospice care so fast? I was not ready to talk to that woman. I asked her to leave and give me a few minutes to be with my family. My classmate from Spelman College sang, "God Will Take Care of You." Our priest prayed for us, and I was ready to talk to the hospice representative.

Along with me, our children and grandchildren, Godson and our priest surrounded Bill's bed. My Godson sang, "A City Called Heaven." Our priest administered last rites. I held Bill's hand and rested the other on his head. I kissed his forehead and whispered, "I love you to death." Bill was settled in hospice care by two o'clock that afternoon.

My head spun. I could not understand how all of this happened so fast. I went to bed the night before happy and prepared to go to work the next day. *I could not believe this was happening! Hospice?* I felt like my heart was being wrenched from my chest.

As the night went on, we received family and visitors who brought food. I felt loved and supported by so many. It was wonderful to know that I had people around. We prayed, cried, laughed at some of the funny things Bill would say and do, and loved on each other. The outpouring shown was a true testament to the fact that everyone loved and respected Bill.

As night came and visitors left, I continued to sit by Bill's bed and hold his hand. His breathing was labored and difficult. It seemed like his whole body was fighting to breathe. I stayed the night with Bill.

I reminisced about the wonderful life he and I had had over the 38 years we had been married and the 43 years we had known each other. I thought about all of the things we had done together. We raised a family. We traveled to six of the seven continents. We went to church and served together in the choir and on several committees. We served as licensed lay ministers and took communion to the sick and shut-in members. We went on a mission trip to Nicaragua and helped lay the foundation for a dormitory. We celebrated our 25th Wedding Anniversary in grand style. We had Easter Egg hunts for our grandchildren and friends each year. We did cross-country road trips and saw 38 states, including Hawaii. We had planned to drive through all 50. Bill *loved* to drive.

I listened to Bill's breaths. One of the assistants told me that Bill was actively dying and would have longer periods of suspended breathing until he stopped altogether. This put me on high alert for his breathing patterns. I was afraid every breath he took would be his last. As irrational as it sounded, I thought being hypervigilant would cause it to continue and prolong his life.

I prayed that if it was God's will to bring Bill back to me, I would be happy to have a few more years with him. After all, I do believe in miracles. I prayed for God's will to be done. I prayed that God would give me the strength to accept God's will in this current situation. I prayed that Bill was not afraid or troubled as he transitioned. I prayed for the Holy Spirit to guide him safely to heaven. I prayed for me and my future without Bill. I prayed that God would continue to take care of me. I prayed and prayed and prayed all through that night.

I rested for short moments on the vacant bed due to my high adrenaline level. I persevered during the night because there was a presence in the room with us. It had to be the Holy Spirit watching over us.

Bill lived through the night. By eight in the morning, I noticed Bill's hand was not as warm as it had been, even though he was still breathing with great difficulty. I knew at that moment that I had to release him. I stood up and leaned close to his ear. I thanked him for giving me a beautiful family. I thanked him for affording me a wonderful life. I said to him it was okay to leave. "I will miss you terribly, but I will be alright." I prayed for God to take him because I did not want to see Bill struggle any longer.

At nine, our daughter returned to the facility. I still held Bill's hand, watching, listening, and praying. I was waiting for his next breath, and I waited, no breath. I put my hand on his chest and realized that Bill was gone about 20 minutes after I told him I would be okay. The nurse pronounced Bill dead at 9:26 a.m. on March 16, 2017. I was still holding his hand when he took his last breath. It was truly amazing. Sometimes, when I remember the moment, I still feel his hand in mine.

My daughter and I called everyone we had seen the day before and many others to inform them that Bill had passed. A few people came to hospice to see Bill in repose and to check on me. I was alright at that moment because I felt a sense of relief that Bill was not suffering anymore, and the fact that he was gone had not sunk in. I, the widow, was calm enough to console some distraught visitors. Imagine that!

In hospice, the staff gave us all the time we needed with Bill after his death. I could not stop touching his forehead because it was still warm, and he seemed asleep. It took a long time for his body to cool. Our priest came for the third time and prayed over Bill and for our family. Then, the most difficult part of my life began.

Living Through the Grief

Initially, I did not know which way to go or how to proceed. I was numb. I had to find a way to move forward.

In the first few weeks, I was very busy with the business surrounding a death. There was so much to do. I had to contact family, friends, and insurance companies. There was the planning for Bill's memorial service. I spoke to funeral directors, printers of his program, and participants. Made special arrangements with florists and musicians, planned a repast, and so much more. Thank God for the busy work because it kept my mind occupied, and I did not have to focus on Bill's death.

Ironically, one's mind can compartmentalize activities and thoughts, protecting the individual from painful issues. I believe this is God's way of protecting us from devastating loss. God gives us a buffer in the early days of loss. He allows our spirits a temporary respite.

Some activities that helped me cope with and live through the grief are listed below.

Prayer- I prayed unceasingly whenever I felt troubled, sad, or needed strength, peace, joy, and general well-being. While there were times my prayers were long, I had brief ones, too. "Have mercy, Jesus; Deliver me, Father; Come Holy Spirit; Help me, Lord; Thank you, Jesus; Spare me this pain, dear God." These prayers made me feel closer to God, giving me the strength to live.

Romans Chapter 8 saved my life and my sanity. I advise everyone reading this essay to read this chapter, with special emphasis on verse 28 and verses 35 – 39.

My father modeled how to go into widowhood with dignity and grace. My parents had been married for forty-nine and a half years. My father was sad and missed my mother but was not devastated. I asked him, "How are you so calm and at ease during Mother's death?" He responded, in essence, "I was prepared for this. I thought about life without her and how I would cope. I prayed I would rejoice in the thought that I had had a wonderful, love-filled life with a lovely woman." He continued, "We did not come here to stay." He ended our conversation with the following scripture, which he repeated from memory; "And we know that in all things God works for the good of those who love Him, who have been called according to his purpose." – Romans 8:28. I was speechless and in awe of my father. He ministered to me. I never forgot that conversation. It was a sermon that he delivered to me in his grief. What a blessing!

Scripture and Devotionals were key. The first thing I did before starting my day was to read scripture and write. This habit sustained me through each day. I read in solitude early before I heard the news of the day. I have at least three published devotionals that I draw from. I begin by reading and meditating on the scripture recommended for the accompanying narrative. Then I read the narrative. Afterward, I would ruminate about the scriptures and narratives. Finally, I pray about what I have read and how I could put it into action.

<u>Family</u> was a God-given blessing that surrounded me. In the first weeks after Bill's death, I had people to visit, call, and reach out via social media. Some managed telephone calls and relayed information about Bill's death and subsequent memorial service so I could rest. This saved me from having to say *it* repeatedly. Friends brought food, food, and more food so that eating was not a concern for us in my home. They even brought goodies and snacks for my grandchildren. I was overwhelmed by the outpouring of love and care from everyone. I felt blessed. I wanted for nothing.

My Godson called me every night, without fail. He checked on my emotional and physical health. We talked until I fell asleep. These late-night calls helped me to calm down from the busyness of each day. He made me laugh about things that had happened at his work, funny interactions with people we knew, and so much more. Our talks helped me to not focus on my empty bed. I looked forward to his call each night. These conversations were very uplifting and special to me.

Finally, I was showered with love from people all over the United States and the world. Calls came from Nicaragua, The Democratic Republic of the Congo, and South Africa.

<u>Music</u> became my refuge and my strength. I was already entrenched in music before I became a widow. I sang with my church choir and a semi-professional, multicultural chorus. I listened to all types of music. For me, music was healing. It transported me to places of comfort, joy, peace, happiness, and appreciation, to name a few. I was lifted out of my grief when I sang or listened to music for a while. It was truly remarkable how music did and does transform me in times when I might be in despair. Thank God for music. And thank God for giving me a voice to sing His praises.

Poetry played a major part as I grieved. I never wrote poetry before my husband died. Then, after his death, I wrote poems on several occasions. The process of writing was an amazing one. The words come from above me, down through my body, and then down onto the paper. It is miraculous. I have to write the words as they come down on me immediately. If not, the words are gone forever. That's why I keep paper and pen with me at all times. Writing poetry is cathartic. It has a comforting effect on those who are grieving.

Work came to my rescue. Returning as a widow filled me with peace. I am a professional librarian by trade and training. I work in an elementary school Media Center. I could spend a whole day assisting children with reading, helping them find a good book, and conducting Pre-Kindergarten story time. In addition, being around team members who were sympathetic, kind, and understanding was wonderful. My job helped with my process because I did not have to be home all day, missing Bill.

Talk therapy was instrumental in helping me deal with stress. Several weeks into widowhood, I needed professional help. I was faring well, but sometimes, I needed to go deeper into my loss. I needed coping skills. The only way, I thought, to get those skills was therapy. I am so happy I went to see a counselor because I needed *a lot* of help.

As the counselor led me through my grief, I did not realize I would be so emotional. Tears, tears, and more tears. I thought I had passed that point. Then, I realized I had been suppressing my emotions and thoughts. I was in the perfect place to let my feelings out. I understood I had tried to be strong for my family and neglected myself. The counselor gave me imagery to help me through my most difficult moments. I advise anyone who has been through a traumatic experience to consider talk therapy. It helped me tremendously.

Moving Toward Acceptance

Moving toward acceptance of widowhood has been the most challenging phase. The reality is that nothing will ever be the same. Life is different. The challenge is to embrace the transformation and incorporate it into daily life. It is important to know that life goes on, and we must move on. To do this, I meditate and rely on the following scriptures.

"This the day the Lord has made; let us rejoice and be glad in it." Psalm 118:24 (NIV)

"For you created my inmost being; you knit me together in my mother's womb. I praise you because I am fearfully and wonderfully made; your works are wonderful. I know that full well." Psalm 139:13-14 (NIV)

"The Lord is my light and my salvation – whom shall I fear? The Lord is the strength of my life – of whom shall I be afraid?" Psalm 27:1 (KJV)

"Wait on the Lord; be of good courage, and he shall strengthen thine heart. Wait, I say, on the Lord." Psalm 27:14 (KJV)

"But seek first his kingdom and his righteousness, and all these things will be given to you as well. Therefore do not worry about tomorrow, for tomorrow will worry about itself…." Matthew 6:33-34 (NIV)

The preceding scriptures are the basis for how I live my life now. Some words and phrases that are important to me as I think about these scriptures are strength, salvation, thankfulness, praise, fearfully and wonderfully made, courage, trust in God, and not worrying about tomorrow. These are reassurances that keep me going from day to day.

I was hurt and sorrowful when my husband died, but I was not devastated or worried. I understood that I was blessed to have loved and been loved by my wonderful husband. What I understand is that we did not come here to stay. I know I will see my husband again when I transition. I know Bill will meet me as I cross over. I am looking forward to this reunion. It will be glorious.

Our life on earth is temporary. Love is eternal. Our approach to death must be based on our Christianity, trust in God, and love of Jesus Christ. In the meantime, I rejoice in the smallest things now: my family, a bird flying in midair, the beautiful faces of my grandchildren, stunning blossoming flowers, bird songs, trees and their perfectly shaped leaves, delicious food, melodic music, and the kindness of others.

Finally, I am a survivor and a conqueror. God still has so much more for me to do. I am looking forward to what God has in store for me. I am ready to follow Jesus wherever He leads.

LOVE IS ETERNAL

A short poem

Love has no end.

Love has no boundaries.

Love has no limitations.

Love reaches high and low.

If you go to the heavens, love is there.

If you go to the depths of the ocean, love is there.

If death separates us, love is STILL there.

Wherever you are, there is love because the creator of the universe is Love.

February 5, 2018

I Wanna Go Home
By Roberta Jackson

It was May 2001, a few days before Memorial Day. I stood beside the hospital bed and watched my mother's fragile body lying there. The television was on the Turner Broadcasting Network, and my father and siblings were in the waiting room. The nurses were entering Mama's room like a busy intersection. I looked away bewildered and silently asked, "How did we get here?"

I was jolted back when my mother tapped my hand twice. I realized the nurse was gone. I looked down at her skinny face with her big brown eyes looking up at me with one of the saddest stares I had ever seen. She said in her hoarse, raspy voice, "I wanna go home." I said, "I know Mama." There was nothing I could do. I didn't have the power to grant Mama her heart's desire.

My mother and I didn't have a close relationship in my younger years. I felt she didn't understand me, nor did I her. We were two distant planets from different galaxies, and there would be even more distance between us in the years to come.

I'm the youngest of two sons and three daughters born to Frankie Robertson. We are all Grady Babies. If you're an Atlanta, Georgia native, you know that means Grady Hospital was the only place a minority child could be born.

The summer before I started 9th grade, my mother started going to church, dragging me and my siblings with her. Before then, we had never gone to church as a family. We started attending church on Saturdays and bible study on Wednesdays. It became an issue between her and me because my high school sporting events fell on those days. Thankfully, my father ran interference, and my athletic years didn't come to a screeching halt.

I loved playing sports (track, basketball, and volleyball) at school and church from the 6th - 12th grades. My siblings came out when they could, and unfortunately, my father didn't attend any events. He was a hard worker with little time for anything else. Sports brought me joy, fulfillment, worth, accomplishment, and satisfaction. To sum it up, sports were my whole world. As a young adult, I played on the women's basketball team at church for many years; I even coached for one year. I got this extreme love of sports from my father; he understood me. He excelled in four different sports in high school.

My mother never played organized sports, nor was she particularly interested in them, but she grew to love bowling. She and my dad even bowled together in leagues for many years. But she was more of an intellectual and loved the arts, especially music and singing. She was accepted into Spelman College and desired to become an Opera singer, but she decided to put her family first.

My mother was very active in the music ministry at church. She was in the choir, and she performed solos. She'd sing nonstop in the house. I admit, I, too, loved singing, and I sang as well, but where no one could hear me. But one day, when she heard me, she told me I needed to join the choir. I sat in a few rehearsals, caught the singing bug, and joined the choir in the 10th grade. It was exciting and scary at the same time. Sports came easy. I was natural at it. Singing, on the other hand, took a lot more effort and practice. My Mama would say, "You're my daughter. You can do it!"

Scales were lifted from my eyes each time she said that. I saw that my mother was trying to connect with me, and other instances would pop up in my mind. Before this, I didn't feel a connection. I finally saw how she was always there for me, even in her absence and when it seemed like I was putting sports before God. My mother loved me with the love of God. Her love wasn't conditional; it was unconditional!

Little did I know that God would use music as a tool to start pulling our planets into the same galaxy.

We were inseparable as we sang and sat by each other in the alto section. We practiced together, and we frequently talked about music. We shared a heart of worship and a desire to be used by God with the gifts He had given us. I could see the pride and joy in her smile and eyes when we sat or stood next to each other as we sang in unity. But outside of the choir, we were still worlds apart. I didn't know my mother, and she didn't know me; I did not let her into my world because I didn't think she would understand me.

My mother came out to my final church track meet when I was a senior in high school. She was very proud of me and wished she had come to the other meets after seeing me run. She couldn't stop talking about my form and my performance. Although the medals were extremely important, I realized that my mother's presence, approval, and joy meant more. I hid my tears of joy. During her excitement, I could see a brief look of sadness as she reflected on how many years of events she had missed. I was so grateful she finally saw me as track was my greatest love.

Several years after graduating high school, I married and moved to another state. I had no family there. Those were times that made me reflect and truly appreciate what I had. I started calling Mama and sharing parts of my life with her. I would have never guessed that the physical miles apart would bring us closer in a new way. The gravitational pull between our two planets drew us closer together.

Years passed, and I got a divorce. Mama was there with open arms to lend a hand, an ear, and her heart in my time of need. We truly became inseparable over the years in a much deeper way. I never would've thought that, as an adult, my mother would become my best friend. Finally, our two planets were in the same system revolving around the sun.

Once again, I sat next to my mother in the alto section of the church choir. It was as if God turned off the noise and clutter in my mind, and let me tell you, there was no better place to be. I had such a sweet, peace singing in the choir. But little did we both know that God had plans for us both individually and together some years down the line. But first, the unexpected and unthinkable would happen.

I stayed at my parents' house while adjusting to a new job and getting back on my feet. Life had more downs than ups as I navigated through my new norm. But I was still determined to be optimistic, with a song on my lips, praise in my heart, daily bible study, and lifting prayers to God. I knew without this, I would not make it to the other side.

One day after work, I noticed that my mother's demeanor had changed, and she seemed concerned and worried. I asked her what was going on. She slowly said, "I have Breast Cancer." My heart dropped. I went numb. I couldn't speak. I thought to myself, *"Did I hear her correctly*?" I yelled, *"Breast Cancer*!" Mama admitted, "I have known for some time, and I'm going the natural route, and I have not told anyone else." My whole world came tumbling down as all sorts of emotions flooded my mind and heart. I started crying and thinking, *"Not my mother! How could this be? We just reunited!"* She pulled me in, and we hugged for what seemed like hours. I think I would have fallen over if Mama had not grabbed me when she did. Mama reassured me that God had her and she'd be okay. Mama was praying and believing God for her healing. I told her I would, too.

In the following days, I proudly thought, *"I was witnessing one of the strongest women I know*." Mama prayed for healing, had daily bible study, continued singing in the choir, and cared for herself. After work, I would help Mama out as much as I could. This was our weekly routine. I'm not sure when Mama told my other siblings. She only told those closest to her at church. We all prayed in agreement with Mama for healing. Daily, we spoke life (words of encouragement) and reminded her of God's unfinished plans. Mama was a blessing to all that she came in contact with.

Five years later, God brought someone special into my life. Tyrone loved my two sons, Tommie and Isaac as if they were his own. My mother adored Tyrone, and he adored my mother. Within a year, we were married. We both agreed to live with my parents so that I could continue to help my mother out.

As time passed, Mama went from being a 5'8, 250+ pound woman to about a hundred pounds or less. It was unbearable to see her like that. I was strong in her presence but cried occasionally while alone in my room. This was truly a heavy load to bear. A new marriage, a new job, and caring for my mother. Tyrone helped when he could (outside of his busy schedule) and prayed fervently for my mother and my strength.

With each passing day, no matter how Mama felt, she allowed God to use her, and he used us both simultaneously. Tyrone was now our choir director. He created a praise team, and we sang on it. We became praise and worship leaders and sang solo pieces or solos within the choir. We even traveled to a ministerial conference in Jekyll Island, Georgia with the praise team. Mama was too weak to participate by this time, but she wanted to take the trip, so we gladly brought her.

A few weeks later, Mama stopped going to church. That decision was one I could tell was weighing on her heavily. I could see it in her eyes and her energy level. But she knew God was still with her, whether she was at church or not. She missed serving Him at church, blessing others with song, praying with members, and fellowshipping. That's what she lived for; that was her whole world.

There was a void in my church life now without my Mama by my side. But I pressed on with prayer. I sat with Mama every Sunday after church, telling her about the sermon, musical selections, announcements, and communicating personal messages from her church family. It felt like we sat for hours. She looked forward to this time, and I did as well. It was truly a highlight of my week to make her smile and happy, if only for a few hours.

Mama purchased an upright piano years before the cancer. She placed it in the living room, teaching herself how to play, and even gave her grandkids lessons before and after the cancer diagnosis. Tyrone would come home from work, sit at the piano, and start playing. Mother would walk downstairs with the biggest smile as he gave her a concert of praise and jazz songs. Sometimes, she would even sing along. However, when she got too weak, she would listen from her bedroom upstairs and sing along with the music, clap with joy, or just scream out with elation as loud as she could. On one hand, I thank God for Tyrone being such a wonderful blessing to our mother. However, on the other hand, it broke my heart to hear how a once soulful, strong alto voice with a three-octave range could be reduced to a cracking and sometimes whispering voice. It brought tears to my eyes and, at times, also to Tyrone's eyes. He even recorded her singing. These were truly very special moments that we will never forget. We both thank God for them.

Mama had to go to the hospital several times to receive fluids, and eventually, the hospital recommended hospice care. Nevertheless, we would all praise God and believe for a miraculous healing of Mama. Despite hospice being in the home, we kept speaking life over Mama and reminded her about all that she still had to do.

She clung to her favorite scriptures:

The LORD is my shepherd; I lack nothing. He makes me lie down in green pastures; he leads me beside quiet waters; he refreshes my soul. He guides me along the right paths for his name's sake. Even though I walk through the darkest valley, I will fear no evil, for you are with me; your rod and your staff, they comfort me. You prepare a table before me in the presence of my enemies. You anoint my head with oil; my cup overflows. Surely, your goodness and love will follow me all the days of my life, and I will dwell in the house of the LORD forever." Psalm 23:1-6 (NIV)

When Mama became too weak to walk alone, I gave her a porcelain handbell to ring whenever she needed me. Some nights were really rough, and I cried, but I pressed on to answer the bell because I loved my Mama, and she needed my help. Tyrone's heart went out to both of us during this period that lasted for months.

Two weeks before May 24th, Mama took some medicine that made her hoarse. This was the first medicine she had ever taken. I knew she had to be in a lot of pain. After she took it, it was hard to understand what she was saying at times, which frustrated her. But she tried her best to communicate.

About a week later, it was a Wednesday when I came home from work, and mother was depressed. I asked her what was going on. She then poured out her heart to tell me all that was weighing so heavily on her as she cried. My heart just broke as she spoke from the depths of her heart, crying for those she loved. As she spoke, she started talking about me and how she felt when she first found out she was pregnant with me. She had four children already, and life was very hard. Mama couldn't imagine how they would take care of five children. I could see how she felt guilty about her thoughts as she wept. I was shocked and confused by her words, and I decided not to take anything personally, even though it was hard, so I prayed to God on the spot.

She closed her eyes and laughed like I had never heard before. And she had the biggest smile and said, "I can see God using you! God's going to use you, and I can't wait to see it!" Then she opened her eyes, and instantly, she was sad again. I felt like, in that very moment, God showed her something that gave her hope in the midst of her hopelessness. That moment has stayed with me. I held tight to her words with anticipation and believed God was faithful to bring whatever He showed her to pass.

With the Memorial Day weekend fast approaching, Tyrone and I made plans to go out of town to visit some family. We were excited about getting away. My sisters would come by to check on Mama while we were gone. I felt slightly guilty for leaving Mama but knew it was for the best.

The Thursday before the holiday started as a regular day. We got up and prepared for work. I helped Mama out before I left. When I got home, I noticed Mama seemed tired and out of it, more than normal. My daddy told me how she had been sleeping a lot all day. I fixed her something to eat, and she ate a little as I told her about my day. Later, Tyrone came home, and she was lethargic when he checked on Mama. I called my siblings, and we decided to take her to the hospital.

Once there, the doctor said she needed fluids and that he would draw some blood and run tests. We were told that only one person at a time could go into her room. We all patiently and yet anxiously awaited our turn. When one person returned, they gave the others an update. It calmed our spirits just a little. It was finally my turn. As I walked down the hall, I continued to pray for peace and words of comfort for Mama and Holy Spirit's leading.

I felt a chill from the cold room as I walked inside. A nurse took blood from my mother's left arm as she closed her eyes tightly and grimaced in pain from the needle. My heart ached for her. I felt so helpless. The nurse left, and the television was on the Turner Broadcasting Network. One of Mama's favorite stations. I then looked back at Mama, and she just looked up at me with her big, sad, looking eyes, and I asked, "*How are you doing*?" She didn't answer me but stared off into space with a blank stare. I then walked over to her, rubbed her soft, silver, and black afro as I spoke life, and reminded her that God was with her.

Then, another nurse entered the room to check her vitals, and Mama stared at me. I had to turn away; I couldn't take her stare anymore without breaking down and crying. As I looked away, I could see two Mamas in my mind. I could see my healthy, vibrant mother before me, and then I saw this fragile woman I barely recognized, although I witnessed her change daily before my eyes. When I glanced back, the nurse was leaving the room.

The man on the television program suddenly announced a singer. Mama's face lit up like I had not seen in a long time. She shouted out loud, "That's Mahalia Jackson!" Then came a video of her singing "Somebody Bigger Than You and I." This was one of Mama's favorite songs. I said to myself, *"Look at God! He's showing her that He's still with her."* As I watched television with joy and praising God, I felt Mama tap me on my left hand two times. Her face was so skinny, and her big brown eyes had one of the saddest stares I had ever seen. She spoke in her hoarse, raspy voice, "I wanna go home." I was at a loss for my own words. She was just enjoying one of her favorite singers singing one of her favorite songs. I slowly said, "I know, Mama, you're going home after the doctors run their test." Mama then gave me a look of disbelief and shook her head frantically from side to side three times. She tapped my hand again with a hard stare and spoke authoritatively, "I wanna go home!" We locked our eyes for a few seconds, but it felt longer. Then I saw beyond the surface, and I understood- *Mama wasn't telling me she wanted to go back to her physical home - but she was asking me for permission to let go so she could go to her eternal home to be with God.*

I closed my eyes, let out a deep breath, and said, "*Mama, you can go home.*" She let out the same laugh she did a week prior when she told me God would use me. Mom turned her head, with the biggest smile on her face, towards the television to watch Mahalia sing. She was at peace. As I stood there in confusion, I reflected on her talk with me and realized I hadn't heard her correctly. What Mama said was, "I can see God using you! God's going to use you, and I wish I could see it." I missed the last part. God knew I couldn't handle it until now. I knew this moment was between Mama and me, and I didn't have the heart to tell everyone else.

I pondered, *Is it selfishness or love to ask a loved one or friend to keep fighting at their lowest moment?* I know each case is different, and only those involved can answer this question. I know letting them go when they are ready is the right thing to do. I must press on through the pain of loss. I've asked myself many times, "*Why was I Mama's chosen one?*" I don't know the answer, but I'm glad I had the kind of relationship where she entrusted me with her heart-wrenching plea. She brought me into this world and asked me if she could leave it.

A few hours later, Mama was released, and we went home. I had a dilemma. Tomorrow, Tyrone and I were heading out of town, and I couldn't leave Mama, knowing it was only a matter of time before she left us. When we were alone. I pleaded with her to let me stay and told her I didn't want to go. She firmly voiced her wishes, "Roberta, you have to go." I pleaded with her to let me stay, and once again, she firmly voiced her wishes, "Roberta, you have to go. You have plans, and you need to be there." I reluctantly agreed, "Okay, Mama. I love you." She said, "I know you do, and God blessed me with a Roberta because He knew I would need you." I cried as I went into the room to pack my bags.

That night was a sobering one. I jumped each time the handbell rang, and even when it didn't, I thought it did. Deep down, I wanted it to ring even more that night than it had any other night before. In my heart, I knew this would be my last night to serve my mother in this capacity, and after tonight, the handbell would be silenced.

The next morning, I fixed Mama breakfast, and we prayed. I told Mama again about my reservations about going on the trip. Mama said, "Roberta, you have to go, and I will be here when you get back." But deep down inside, I didn't think I would. I bent over and carefully hugged Mama goodbye as she lay in the hospice bed, and I kissed her forehead. I softly rubbed my fingers through her soft, silver, and black afro, and I said, "I love you, Mama," and Mama said, "I love you, Roberta." Then I left the room.

The ride down the interstate was quiet as I reflected on my journey with my mother. I cried, I chuckled to myself, and I prayed. A couple of hours into the trip, I had to let my thoughts of Mama go and be in the present moment for Tyrone. He, too, had been through a lot during this journey with Mama. His first year of our marriage so far had been sharing his wife with his ill mother-in-law. I truly thank God for blessing me with such a special man because he sacrificed a lot for us.

We arrived at our destination, settled in, and visited our family. My heart was still heavy, but I prayed that God would strengthen and help me be in the moment. We had a good Friday and Saturday. I made sure I checked in on Mama both days, and she was fine.

We were preparing to leave for church on Sunday morning, and the phone rang in our hotel room. It was the eeriest sound I had ever heard. Then, a feeling came over me, and I knew. I just knew. Tyrone answered the phone. As he relayed the message, he started crying, "Your Mama passed this morning." I cried like a baby as he held me. I said, *"I knew she was going to die while I was gone; she knew it, and that's why she pushed me away, so I wouldn't be there to see it,"* We gathered our things and got on the road back to Atlanta.

That five-hour trip was the longest trip I had ever taken. Tyrone and I talked, laughed, cried, reminisced about our journey with Mama, and spoke about regrets and thanksgiving. This journey united Tyrone and me in a way we never saw coming. But God! God orders steps, and He knows how much we can bear. He knew I needed to remember seeing my mother alive, even in her weakest state. Deep down, I believe Mama asked God to take her when I left for the same reason.

Once at the house, my sister told me with tears and disbelief what happened and how she found Mama not breathing in the bed when she went back to check on her. Daddy was understandably numb and in tears. I had never seen him like that before. Time stood still, and I don't recall the details of that day after getting the horrific details from my traumatized sister.

In the coming days, we planned for Mama's "Celebration of Life" service. Mama was 1 of 13 children, and several siblings were asked to participate in the service. My siblings asked me to sing because Mama loved my voice and because we sang together. I didn't have the courage to sing, but I told them I would write and recite a poem. I prayed about the poem, and God led me to read one I had written years prior. He also led me to speak before reading the poem.

A CHRISTIAN SOLDIER

***A CHRISTIAN SOLDIER** is what I am called,*
To endure with courage and never fall.
I might stumble now and then, so back I go to war again.
To march to war without fear, to always know that God is near.

***A CHRISTIAN SOLDIER** must wear his whole armor,*
If he is going to conquer.
One piece or two will never do; you better place it all over you.
He must stay on guard day and night, be diligent,
and vigilant during his fight.
He goes to war daily, so he has no time to become lazy.
He knows his enemy is wise and tricky,
so he must think very quickly.
He must never let the wrong thoughts stay in but cast them out lest he sin.

***A CHRISTIAN SOLDIER** must constantly take orders,*
Only from his High Authority.
He must follow them totally and not go half-heartedly.
He must never grow weary in times of trouble,
Just remember he has got cover.

***A CHRISTIAN SOLDIER** is what I am,*
I must endure until the end because I am ordered.
When the war is finally over, of course, the soldier is the winner,
His commander will then say,
"WELL, DONE, MY GOOD AND FAITHFUL SERVANT!"
By Roberta Jackson - Spring 1988

It was a wonderful Celebration of Life for Mrs. Frankie Mae Keepler Robertson. One filled with songs, joy, love, tears, laughter, and reflections. Tyrone put together a recording that featured songs with Mama singing; it played before the service. I felt peace when I went to the podium to speak. A spirit of boldness came over me. When I sat down, I was overwhelmed with emotions, and a typhoon of tears poured from my eyes, and then I was okay. At the gravesite, a minister friend told me I was a very strong woman to have done what I did. I thanked him, knowing God brought me through.

I've learned from this experience to be more observant of loved ones or friends who are ill or even on the verge of dying. I must pray for discernment to read into what they are saying or not saying and even read their body language. I also learned to be present and just sit in silence if that's what's needed or just be an ear to listen to their hearts cry. Finding common ground with them is very important. Although we may not have the same interests, there's always a commonality, such as love, drive, and resilience. There must be a desire and determination to find that correlation between us. We all have to get out of our comfort zone, and then we might see we have more in common than we think.

Tyrone and I lived with my father for one more year as he adjusted to his new life. Then we moved out, and my oldest brother was with him. I didn't know what tomorrow held for me, but I knew God showed Mama something, and I've been hanging onto that promise ever since. I miss Mama tremendously, even 22 years later and counting. But I know without a doubt that she's with the Lord, with no pain, and one day, I will see her again in her flawless body! God knew I needed a Frankie... My Mama... My Best Friend!

"For I know the plans I have for you, declares the Lord,
plans to prosper you and not to harm you,
plans to give you hope and a future."
Jeremiah 29:11 (NIV)

Working Through Career Challenges

"Never allow a person to tell you 'no' who doesn't have the power to say 'yes'."

~Eleanor Roosevelt, U.S. First Lady, Diplomat and Activist

"We can do anything we want to do if we stick with it long enough."

~Helen Keller, Author, Disability Rights Advocate, and Lecturer

"Challenges make you discover things about yourself that you never really knew."

~Cicely Tyson, Award Winning Actress

eorgia State
University
COLLEGE
OF LAW

Navigating the Path to My Best Self
By Gail Tusan Washington

There is an expression, "Let your hater be your motivator." As I reflect, I realize that, at times, this has been true for me. Some of my best achievements have been accomplished in the wake of someone underestimating my abilities and spawned by my determination to prove them wrong.

I have always had an idea of what I want to do and generally understood how to get there. Those who know me best would likely describe me as a planner, organizer, and take-charge person. In large measure, I have experienced success in my endeavors. But that is not to say success has come easy for me or that things have gone according to my plan. Nor should it. I have encountered my share of obstacles, naysayers, and disappointments. People, circumstances, and self-doubt have emerged along my path as roadblocks. Some challenges seemed bigger than others when I faced them.

I share my story with the hopes that regardless of which phase of life's journey you may be in, you will take away a tiny gem to help navigate past any roadblocks or obstacles. We know they are out there, and we rarely have the luxury of anticipating them to avoid them completely. That leaves us only to mentally prepare for all things being possible and, when encountering an impediment, to be guided by our inner voice, which rarely leads us astray.

Pardon me, Ma'am, I am not interested in Food Services

On a crisp early spring day, I entered the white Human Resources trailer down the hill behind the ticket booth, where visitors lined up awaiting admission for their tour of Universal City Studios. Despite my nervousness, I felt confident that I was tour guide material. Ever since my mother took my brother and me on a tour to see how the movie, *JAWS*, was made, I set my sights on becoming a tour guide someday. The coveted position at Universal

Studios requires a working knowledge of the inner mechanisms of the more than 400-acre Hollywood studio and the ability to answer questions from hungry fans about their favorite T.V. shows, movies, and actors. I completed the long application, highlighting my high school scholastic and extracurricular achievements, personal references from church, community service, and the local library where I had worked through high school. As my freshman year at UCLA was well underway, I proudly checked the box asking about post-secondary education. I turned in my application to the receptionist, and after what seemed like forever, an older white woman appeared from an interior office and called my name. I will never forget hers. I followed R.B. and took a seat as she sat behind her desk.

"Your application does not list any theatrical or stage production experience. So why do *you* want to be a tour guide?" she asked. Her emphasis on *you* suggested she couldn't fathom how I envisioned myself at the front of a tram, holding a microphone and entertaining and educating tourists worldwide about the ins and outs of filmmaking. I resisted the urge to remind her that the job announcement stressed the importance of strong interpersonal skills, work experience in the public sector, and outgoing personalities. Neither acting experience nor film credits were listed as requirements. As a top student, engaged in student government and a myriad of community service endeavors, a Camp Fire Horizon Club member, and a youth leader at my church, I did not share R.B.'s skepticism about my qualifications. My village had instilled in me the values of self-reliance and confidence. I was prepared for this opportunity. I knew I could not simply perform the job but, with preparation and on-the-job experience, would excel while doing it.

"I enjoy working with people, and as a psychology major, I am looking for new opportunities to interact with the public," I responded.

"There's much more to being a tour guide than simply liking people," she snapped. Despite her piercing negative air, I nodded, trying to keep my high hopes inflated. "The process for becoming a tour guide is highly competitive. I am not sure that you are aware that there is an exam you would need to pass, testing your knowledge of the information provided by our guides during the tours." I was warned. "I think you should consider a position in our Food Services division instead. They have several openings, and I could place you immediately. Any interest in taking one of those jobs?"

I shook my head, feeling more determined by the minute to prove my case to the small-minded woman. "Respectfully, Ma'am, if my interest was in food services, several other options are much closer to my home. I would like the opportunity to take the exam, and I feel certain I will pass it." I remembered my father's admonition that saying less is best in certain situations.

Resigned that I would not be talked out of my mission, she gave me the study handbook and scheduled me to return later in the week for the exam. I studied until I was dreaming about sound stages, façades, the special effects enabling Charles Heston to part the Red Sea, Tippi Hedren, all those scary birds, and so much more.

I returned for the tour guide exam and passed it. R.B. hired me despite her shock that I had shattered her initial assessment. I knew my performance would be subject to her scrutiny. However, I refused to let her bias impede my obtaining the incredible experience of working at Universal Studios. I was satisfied that I achieved what I set out to do. I could hardly contain my excitement as I called home with the good news, signed employment documents, put on my brand-new tour uniform, and perused my work schedule.

A bit of drama played out while we waited to be dispatched for our first tours. A rowdy valley girl tour guide *accidentally* coughed up a mouth full of hot chocolate all over my uniform shirt. Apologies and paper towels were offered, but the accident felt intentional and personal to me. At the time, I responded gracefully and headed to the bathroom to clean my shirt. I wondered whether her tackiness was a sign of her resentment for having to work alongside a Black tour guide. If so, the group did not share her intolerance, and before long, our class of tour guides had meshed. My full attention was spent doing my best to give the studio visitors their money's worth. Even though R.B. could never completely overcome her initial prejudgment of me, she afforded me a tremendous learning experience, preparing me for greater opportunities. One of the greatest lessons I took from my experience at Universal Studios is never to accept someone else's view as the barometer of my self-worth. The true measure of who we are and what we can do must come from within.

The Power of Red Ink

Mid-way through my matriculation at UCLA, I took a Philosophy of Law class. It was one of my most interesting classes in college. As a result, I decided that I was more interested in pursuing a law degree (where I could still apply my knowledge of psychology and interpersonal skills) than my original goal of applying to graduate school to become a child psychologist. While growing up, I think the seed for my legal career was planted through my close relationship with three Black lawyers and my observations regarding their passion for public service. When I shared my thoughts with them about modifying my plans for post-college, they enthusiastically encouraged my interest and endorsed my plan to apply to law school. The endorsement of my village was empowering. Becoming the first in my family to become an attorney motivated me. My mentors warned me that law school would be difficult and that my classes and the required study regimen would differ greatly from my college experience. Yet, they reassured me I would succeed and was well suited for a future in the legal profession.

They did not exaggerate about the overall culture shock one encounters as a first-year law student. I was not alone in that regard. The volume of reading required for class preparation was mind-boggling, and class discussions were intense, but I dug in and braced myself for the journey. In addition to the required courses covering various substantive areas of the law, such as contracts, torts, and criminal law, another law school standard for entering students is completing legal research and writing classes. This is where we learn to identify case precedents and legal authorities and acquire the writing skills to advocate persuasively for our future clients. That is, how to draft legal memoranda, motions, and briefs. Excellent legal writing takes lots of practice and refinement. No one arrives at or graduates from law school already having mastered this critical skill.

Within the first few weeks of law school, the biggest threat to my confidence surfaced where I least expected it. I had done very well in my English and writing classes previously. Not only had I excelled and drawn high praise from my high school teachers and college professors, but I truly enjoyed writing. Imagine my despair when my legal writing professor returned my first writing assignment filled with red-inked edits and scathing comments declaring figuratively: "Houston, we have a problem!" He told me that my writing deficits were sufficiently severe and that I likely would not make it through law school. Professor Red Ink did not join R. B. in suggesting I consider a career in the fast-food industry, but he came mighty close.

For most professionals, honing their legal writing continues beyond law school. Strategies to improve one's writing are often topics of ongoing education for new and seasoned attorneys and judges alike. Despite Professor Red Ink's bluntness, I paid attention, put in the necessary hard work, and learned much during my class with him. My hurt feelings did not keep me from appreciating I had a right to be there and to learn from him; his job was to teach me and my classmates, and we did not need to be friends as part of the process. We must never allow someone else's closed perception of our ability to become our reality.

Ironically, years later, after graduating from law school and launching my legal career, I was invited to serve as an adjunct law professor and teach a legal research and writing class. Recalling the traumatic effect of my former professor's preferred pen color, I decided to comment and edit students' submissions using blue ink. More importantly, I remembered how I felt as a law student when subjected to harsh ridicule about my written communication skills. I made a concerted effort to guide my students through the learning process and provide constructive criticism without humiliating or discouraging them. Teaching college and law students has been one of the most rewarding aspects of my career. We must reach back and bring along those coming behind us so that each can become their best self. Again, I was able to take an initial assessment of myself, this time as a less-than-competent writer and propel myself into an effective writer who could impart great writing skills to others.

Making a Bold Choice

When I entered law school, I thought I wanted to be a legal aid attorney – someone who handles legal issues of a civil nature for those unable to afford to pay for legal representation. Three years later, after amassing experience working with a pro bono civil law clinic and significant summer clerk experience with the U.S. Justice Department, graduation was approaching, and I was ready to begin my legal career. My series of job interviews produced a very attractive offer from a prestigious corporate law firm. The opportunity promised top-notch legal training and mentoring, abundant resources and support staff, and access to the best and the brightest of the legal profession. I put a pause on pursuing a legal aid attorney position and accepted the offer. My acceptance made me the first black female associate to be hired by the firm.

Every day, as I entered the lobby of one of Atlanta's tallest skyscrapers and stepped off the elevator on the main floor of the law firm's palatial, majestically decorated office, the sharply dressed, high-energy receptionist greeted me warmly. Despite the sting from my first-day hallway encounter with an elderly name partner and him asking me if I was a new secretary, the overall *need to pinch myself, do I work here* reality test feeling never wore off. I was surrounded by exquisite original artwork (then one of the largest private collections in the Southeast) and luxuriously appointed office suites. Through the large windows of my private office, I could see the city's landscape for miles. The majestic view encouraged daydreaming. But deadlines and demanding supervising partners squashed the temptation. As a brand-new attorney, most of my time was spent in the firm's library conducting legal research or at my desk buried in document review or drafting and revising legal memos and court pleadings. My days were long, often spilling into weekends. The work was tedious, and the pressure to perform was tremendous. The attorneys and the support staff were a team, and each of us played an important part in serving our clients. Most clients were companies, businesses, municipalities, or wealthy individuals with big money issues and legally complex disputes. The work experience I gained at the firm was invaluable.

As billable hour requirements loomed in the air, I realized I would need to seek community service outside of the office to satisfy my desire and law school goal to help ordinary folks with their everyday legal and societal problems. I did not have to look long or far to find ways to serve my community. Atlanta is a hub for volunteerism, community engagement, and philanthropy, and my firm places a high value on being a good corporate citizen. We were encouraged to fulfill our professional obligation to provide pro bono service on top of our billable hours. Community service, pure and simple, spoke to my soul, and I quickly became involved in many pro bono and volunteer activities, including serving as a founding member and second President of the Georgia Association of Black Women Attorneys and President of the Atlanta Legal Aid Society. Admittedly, maintaining a healthy balance between my community service commitments, work responsibilities, and family life as a wife and mother was challenging.

Approximately three years into my law practice, on what started as an ordinary workday, an interoffice phone call interrupted my flow to request that I meet with the firm's managing partner and my mentor. In the impromptu meeting, the sole topic was my future at the firm. While the managing partner commended me for my civic involvement and leadership, my mentor's body language signaled the tone of the discussion was about to change. Then, the managing partner proceeded to spell out his recommendation that I pull back on my community service if my career goal was to work my way up the ladder from employee to partner. I found myself gazing out the window behind him in silent shock. When he finished speaking, I acknowledged I understood the message relayed and excused myself to return to the privacy of my office to process what had just transpired.

After a tearful call to my mother and through prayer and inner reflection, I chose to separate the message from the cynical messenger and accept the gift inherent in the choice he posited. The pause button on my goal of a public service career had been tapped, releasing me to take another step toward my best self and purpose in life. The managing partner was not an obstacle to my future as R. B. or Professor Red Ink had threatened to be. Instead, his unsolicited candor forced me to be honest about my commitment to a professional course that was at odds with my true desire to serve. Once empowered to shift gears, I took stock of my gifts, talents, and passion to serve, and not long after the meeting, I resigned from the firm to pursue other opportunities. Over time, I realized a life balance that afforded me to be true to what was most important and what I wanted: my family and public service.

I am grateful for the core values I received growing up, which enabled me to navigate and overcome roadblocks to achieve my purpose. I now appreciate how certain obstacles propelled me toward a positive resolution. I have learned that how we react to life's impediments is far more important than the fact that we experience them. When my senior partner suggested that I curtail my commitment to public service and I responded by increasing it, I did not know that I would ultimately serve my community as a judge. Little did I know how fulfilling embracing my true purpose would be. I continue to listen to my inner voice. It continues to encourage me to be positive, to think boldly, and to be patient for what is to come.

Invisible Paths
By Henrietta Stith Andrews

"Again and again, we are reminded by the facts of our own lives that there is an aspect of our experience which seems to be beyond our own control, and yet it seems ever to manipulate us into position."
~Howard Thurman, Meditations of the Heart

THE YEARNING BEGINS

The dining room table on Parmelee Avenue was where I was every school day, Monday through Thursday. After the younger siblings were in bed and my parents retired for the day, I sat surrounded by books, pencils, pens, and tablets, struggling with homework, a chore that felt like walking through thick mud with ill-fitting boots. Across the street were single-family homes. Our minister, his wife, and their two sons lived in the house to the left. On more than one late evening, my wavering concentration would be interrupted as I noticed, through the window, ghostly headlights slowly creeping up their driveway, signaling the end of another long day of church work for my pastor and his wife.

During those impressionable teen years of the fifties, these two people awed me – her gifted musical talent, his way with words, their boundless energy, and their selflessness. I admired their dedication. I found myself nurturing a deep longing for some unknown future job that I could not wait to get out of bed for. I imagined this was how they felt about their jobs. A seed was planted.

I understand myself in two distinct ways. They are what I call the outer vestiges of self – what one sees with the eye: I am a woman, a person of color, one with limited resources, a parent, and once a spouse. Throughout my life, these realities have been challenged by other people, laws, shaped by the places I have called home, and ever-changing perspectives. The more I attempt to be independent by not allowing these realities to become roadblocks, the more likely there is resistance along with occurrences that provide what is needed to move ahead on my terms.

The second way I understand myself is through what I refer to as my *inner self* represented in my conscious thought, that voice I have learned to listen to. A voice that I like to believe includes God's voice. My earliest memory of experiencing this inner voice occurred at age eight or nine. I had planned one evening to commit suicide. I was an unhappy child- not abused, simply unhappy, and even as I thought about committing suicide, I was saddened thinking about my parents finding my injured body in the morning. I planned to kill myself with a butcher knife from the kitchen, which was to be accomplished after my parents fell asleep. With the morning light, I realized I missed that opportunity because I had fallen asleep. There was a thought that was suddenly in my thinking. I thought I should go ahead and live to age twenty-five and see what life would be like. I had no idea where that thought came from. In later years, long past the age of twenty-five, I realized the decision to live was not made alone.

A TURNING POINT

It was 5 a.m., mid-June 1966 when I pulled out of the driveway. At the age of twenty-four, I was beginning a trip from Cleveland, Ohio, to Fisk University in Nashville, Tennessee, and driving alone in my 1965 Mustang. Not long after leaving the house, I realized my car radio was not working even though the volume knob was turned up as far as it would go. This was a nuisance, but there was no time to fix the problem, even if I thought I could.

I taught classroom music for the Cleveland Board of Education the previous school year, but I needed a math and a science course to be certified to teach in Ohio. In 1964, when I graduated from Yankton College in South Dakota as a music major, those courses were not required. I chose Fisk University because I wanted the experience of being a student on a Black college campus.

By early afternoon, I was somewhere in Kentucky and tired but determined to stay on the highway rather than risk my safety at local exits in the South. And then the unthinkable happened. I fell asleep at the wheel, driving 70 mph on a divided highway. In my sleep, I passed a truck and then drifted to the right where, at that point on the highway, the land was flat, although rocky. The car bumped until the jarring caused the radio to come on with a blast of sound. That woke me up, and I got the car onto the shoulder. With the assistance of the truck driver, who was a shaken witness, I determined that my car had only minor damage.

I could have died. I could have drifted to the left, crossed the median strip, and met another car head-on. I could have ended up in a river or with my car wrapped around the supports of a bridge. But none of that took place. I reasoned that I had been spared for an unknown future where I imagined God needed me. Before I continued the drive toward Nashville, I embraced the challenges of any future job. I would learn what skills I needed for this unknown work I had been saved for.

DECADES OF VISIONS

Visions or daydreams assume residence
in my thinking for years unbidden.
I have no control
about when they appear,
the details - always the same and
never shared with others.
There is no fear associated with these visions.
There is acceptance – a pondering about their meaning.
I learned early, without understanding,
to simply pay attention and wait.
I realized in time that this is one way God communicates with me.

THE UNFOLDING OF HENRIETTA

In August of 1979, we arrived in Lancaster, Pennsylvania, on the campus of Lancaster Theological Seminary with everything we owned so that my husband, Steve, could begin seminary. Cathy and Stephen Jr. were babies; I would be a mom at home. The seminary campus sits on a city block in a residential area. We lived in seminary housing, which for us was an apartment. We were the only Black family on campus, in our immediate neighborhood, and the only Black family where we worshipped on Sundays.

The plan for the first year was for me to be a stay-at-home mom. I turned my attention to cooking from scratch, providing stability for our family on our shoestring budget, and being a supportive spouse. Then, one day, about a month after we arrived, mid-morning, I reached for an obviously used drinking glass that I thought I had washed about a half hour earlier but, there it was, out of place, needing to be washed again. In that moment, a wave of emotion flooded my being creating a deep longing for all that I left behind. My life felt like a perpetual carousel, and my brain was about to atrophy.

Back home in Cleveland, I worked for the Salvation Army as director of their daycare programs. In seven years of employment, we grew from twenty children to one hundred fifty and from one to two locations. There were challenges, but the reward was being able to help staff grow as individuals and together support the families we served. But that morning, standing in the kitchen of our apartment, I felt like a fish out of water. I was missing the satisfaction I derived from working. I was missing the people and the challenges.

But something new happened. Growing questions about my faith crept into conversations with seminary friends. There was a session with our pastor following his sermon's clear invitation to pay attention to the signs and symbols in our lives. I heard that message and wanted to know more. Was the restlessness and yearning that I was experiencing an example of what I needed to pay attention to?

Those questions marked the beginning of a time I refer to as the unfolding of Henrietta. That period was something like a rosebud that imperceptibly opened up to reveal hidden potential and talents.

Sometime in the early seventies, before we moved to Lancaster and during my employment with the daycare in Cleveland, I began experiencing a vision that continued for a decade. It was like a gentle tap on the shoulder. Pay attention- it seemed to say. The vision was an intrusive mental picture with details that never changed. I had no control over the day or time it would be prominent in my thinking, and I had no idea what the vision meant. In the vision...

I enter a conference room such as one finds in a hotel set up for a lecture- rows of chairs, a center aisle, and a raised stage with a lectern in the center. I enter through a door at the back and center of the conference room, turn to the left, walk to the wall, and turn right toward the front. And as I walk, I realize I am wearing the finest black suit I have ever owned. The closer I get to the front, I realize that I am to be the speaker, and when I arrive at the first row of chairs abruptly, the vision stops.

Whenever Steve's classmates came to our apartment, I longed to be part of their lively discussions that were, I imagined, an extension of a lecture. I was not satisfied to simply serve them whatever refreshment we had to offer. I had thoughts and questions that I wanted to interject. I paused one day in front of Steve's desk, curious- picking up a book – holding it- flipping the pages, wanting to be part of what those words were all about. Once I learned that spouses could audit classes without charge, I decided to audit classes apart from any that Steve took. By the second class, I began participating if the professor allowed my voice to be heard. I had conversations with the campus priest, who was there for the benefit of the students. We talked, but I felt awkward and ill-equipped, lacking the requisite language needed to discuss questions that emerged concerning myself as an *okay* Christian at best. I was thirsty and hungry for a deeper understanding of my faith, including my search for God.

In another vision...

I am standing alone, facing a large window wider than the extensions of both arms. The glass separates me from my view into a room with people seated at a food-filled table. I can see the steam rising from the many dishes and imagine the aromas and the good time the people seated around the table are having. God is on that side of the glass, and my frustration is that I have no way of getting there.

I discovered, at the pace of a turtle traversing a steep incline, that I could write. I began to recognize that when I expressed myself, others were listening and that I was creative. I became more willing to step out of my shell– pull my head out of the proverbial sand and speak up. Qualities of leadership became apparent.

As we neared the end of the first year, my thinking turned to the world of work. We needed me to be employed, but what was I to do? I had a bachelor's in music education and considered teaching music in the public schools in Lancaster. That door was closed the day the official letter of rejection arrived. I considered becoming a music therapist- in a hospital – another path blocked by my failure to follow through.

I ended up working for the YWCA as a lead preschool teacher. It felt strange to be in the classroom rather than supervising the teachers. It was not long before I discovered that I enjoyed the class-room experience without the administrative responsibilities. In those days, I lived with a ukulele in one hand and an autoharp close by. I had a repertoire of kiddie songs to keep a room full of toddlers entertained for nearly an hour. I taught those songs to their mommies. I loved the work.

Questions about my faith still lingered. What was new were the tentative thoughts about me as a seminarian. I had moved from simply attending classes to asking serious questions. I was encouraged by one friend who asked if I ever thought about seminary. "Yes," I said, "but I don't talk about it." She responded that I should give the thought a voice. Another friend said I could be hers if I were a pastor.

On graduation day of 1982, I stood watching members of Steve's seminary class on their way to the chapel. I remember feeling sad. Steve was not graduating as he had not completed the coursework. That day had more to do with my longing for something I imagined was lost. The door was closing, and I felt my connection with the seminary drifting away.

THE PAIN OF DECISIONS

What followed were what I refer to as the in-between years when neither Steve nor I was a student. We lived off campus, one block away, in the middle of a narrow city street of row houses, each separated by a narrow passage that led to the backyard. The kids were in elementary school, and I was now in a supervisory position for the YWCA's Day Care Program and enjoying my work.

Like a shadow that hovered about me throughout those ordinary days were these urgings, these constant thoughts about seminary, and I felt guilty about them. I felt guilty because I was dreaming about what I knew Steve wanted and was having such a difficult time achieving. One Saturday evening, I had a vision.

I was folding clothes alone in the bedroom of our house on that narrow city street. Suddenly and vividly and for no apparent reason, I found myself thinking about the Bible story of Samuel and Eli, where Samuel kept getting up from his mat and going to Eli, believing that Eli had called him. There was no logical reason for me to suddenly think about that story as I had not read it recently, nor had I heard it preached.

There it was, this vision, planted firmly in my conscious thinking. The next morning, we almost did not go to church. At the very last moment, I said to my husband, "Let's go."

I was stunned as the scriptures were read. It was Samuel and Eli, and then the passage about Mary and Martha and the Good Portion from the New Testament. In this story, Jesus refuses Martha's suggestion that he admonish Mary for sitting at his feet learning rather than being in the kitchen. Jesus said that Mary was doing the good portion. She was choosing to sit at the feet of Jesus. In those precious moments- in the sanctuary on that hot August morning -listening to the scripture readings with tears streaming down my cheeks, I knew I was meant to be in church that day. I felt as if I were the only person present in worship. It was as if God was speaking directly to me through those scripture readings. How much clearer did this call to the ministry need to be?

But really, my conscience demanded, how could God close a door for Steve and open that same door for me? That is what it felt like. Competition that I did not ask for. This pull toward ministry was widening the chasm that existed within our marriage. I struggled to overcome the guilt of entertaining the idea of following that call – was I being selfish?

SAYING IT OUT LOUD

One memorable evening in the mid-1980s, during February, I sat with a seminary professor in a basement room of the main building on campus. I was trying to explain this call to ministry that I was experiencing, but the word ministry was not sliding out. This word that needed to be birthed and freed from my imagination into reality was stuck- constricted- a signal that this conversation was of the utmost importance. I finally pushed through- to give voice to what had been lingering in the background for years. He asked if ministry included preaching – did I want to preach, and I quickly answered, "No, I don't want to preach." Then he asked, "What kind of minister do you want to be?" I could not answer this question directly because I had no idea. So, with hesitation, I described a ministry I could well imagine myself doing- one that would utilize the gifts I knew myself to possess. But the ministry I described that night I did not know existed.

When Steve and I talked about my testing this notion of seminary, I proposed that I begin by attending classes designed for lay people interested in church history and theology. He said, "Go for it." He even gifted me with an inscribed Bible, but the truth that night was in his body language that was a clear *no*. In time, I made an independent decision to follow the leading of the Spirit. It seemed so clear the path I needed to follow. It seemed so clear to me that I did not want, in years to come, to regret not following the urgings, which would have meant not listening to that inner voice. It took courage for me to follow the pull on my heart — go to seminary even if the whole world was not on board. At that point, my baggage of being Black, a woman, a mother, a wife, and one with limited finances could no longer serve as roadblocks. It was no longer about being defined by others but rather about following my inner resolve. I needed to move on and trust that all the signs and visions were not leading me astray.

Six months later, I drove to Cleveland, Ohio, for an interview with the Association Minister of the Western Reserve Association. That interview officially began the process toward ordained ministry. I would be in care of an ecclesiastical body that would guide me through the process. I was accountable to them and expected to meet with them in person at least once a year. This body of ministers and laypersons eventually ordained me to ministry on behalf of the United Church of Christ. It might have been easier to be in care with the Association closest to our home in Lancaster. However, our home church was in Cleveland. And I wanted to be ordained in my home church.

What I could not have known during that first interview in Cleveland was that the office where we sat that day was next door to the office that, in about a decade, would be my office. I would be called to a ministry as an Associate Association Minister, similar to what I attempted to describe to the seminary professor six months earlier.

The first evening I sat in a seminary class as a bonified student, I was overwhelmed by emotions. I felt great inner peace, realizing I was where I was supposed to be. I was learning to listen to my inner self and trust the interventions of visions that led me along those otherwise invisible paths. I participated in a workshop with six other seminarians in September of my second year. For a second time in class, I heard myself offering the image of myself standing before a large window, lamenting that God was over there and I could not get there. This second time, the professor asked if I ever considered that God was standing next to me, looking through that glass. What a thought-provoking question! I had for years sought God as inaccessible, never imagining God otherwise. That day and that question halted my search for God outside of myself, and I never experienced that image again.

A year later, I led worship as a seminary student in our home church in Pennsylvania. I had just finished offering the morning prayer at the altar and turned to walk the short distance to the pulpit. In that brief moment, the recurring vision of me walking toward the front of a lecture hall dressed in the finest black suit I ever owned was prominent in my thinking. And suddenly, for the first time, there was understanding. "I'm doing it!" I never had that vision again.

I served the United Church of Christ as an ordained minister for nineteen years. Included in that ministry were the six years I served Ridgeview Congregational Church in White Plains, New York, as their pastor responsible for preaching – the very thing I had said no to. Those years were challenging, but I was prepared and focused on ministry. I approached the totality of ministry with the confidence of one who had moved through doubts and fears and found my path. During that time, my children grew into adulthood and were on their own. I was single, and while I was not wealthy, I was financially stable. I trusted my inner voice and accepted that God and I did ministry together. But the greatest gift was that I loved what I did, and most mornings, I could not wait to get out of bed to start my day.

Accepting Physicality, Aging, and Uncertainty

"It took me quite a long time to develop a voice, and now that I have it, I am not going to be silent."

~Madeleine Albright, Former US Secretary of State

"The great thing about getting older is that you get a chance to tell the people in your life who matter what they mean to you."

~Mike Love, American Singer & Songwriter, and co-founder of the Beach Boys

"Aging is not lost youth, but a new stage of opportunity and strength."

~Betty Friedan, Author The Fountain of Age

SEAT
Welcome
TO THE WEDDING OF
ILA
Please
FIND YOUR

Alopecia Essay
By Tisa Jackson

I yanked at the hinged arm of my husband's shaving mirror. My hands shook as I tried to achieve the right angle to see over my shoulder. Once I got my backward and over-the-shoulder bearings, I could see the first round, smooth patch of skin. It always started this way: one slightly concave, somewhat round bald spot. Other spots would soon appear, with the same indented skin, look and feel. My insides were screaming, "Not again, not now!" I quickly checked my scalp for any more tell-tale spots, scrutinizing every parting for that extra wide-looking appearance. My first thought was to call my dermatologist and make an appointment for cortisone injections. Without thinking, I slid my hand through my hair and back down its fifteen inches of length. This motion was not a useless motion of vanity but born out of the dreadful anticipation of losing copious amounts of hair over time. As my hair ended and fell to my shoulders, softly cascading onto my back, I checked to see how many strands were in my hand and how many were clubbed at the end by a small white bulb. The white bulb is a bundle of protein that helps hair follicles root to the scalp, allowing the hair to grow until it sheds. There were about twenty-plus strands, each clubbed with that little white bulb! I cursed at the mirror, knowing my reflection would confirm my worst fears in about a month.

I've lived with Alopecia most of my life. I have teetered between fearing the worst, total baldness, and hoping for a miraculous cure. Most recently, I've learned that there is no cure for Alopecia. Alopecia is an autoimmune disease that has to be managed by diet and exercise. People like myself who suffer/battle the disease express Alopecia or baldness when our bodies are inflamed. We are beginning to learn that our foods play a major role in managing the inflammation expressed as Alopecia. Each year, I take a physical examination, and then my doctor tells me I'm healthy. Which leads me to question, "If I'm healthy, why am I bald?" Then there's talk of seeing a dermatologist, and it was down the proverbial rabbit hole I'd go. Enduring painful cortisone injections, counting the hairs in my comb and brush, and covering bald spots creatively. The stress of feeling not in control of what's happening would leave me depressed. I would also become hyper-vigilant with shampooing, conditioning, and oiling my hair. I'd absolutely dread the moment that a spot became exposed, and someone tried to nonchalantly hide my secret to save me from embarrassment. Though I am grateful for their attempt to keep me from public humiliation, the act of them securing my secret was embarrassing as hell.

There were times that I was so hyper-focused on the disease and what my outward appearance presented that I did not think to understand what was happening systemically inside my body. Alopecia areata is an autoimmune disease in which a person's immune system goes haywire and attacks body organs and systems, impairing their functions. My immune system confuses my hair follicles to be intruders and chokes them out, resulting in hair loss.

My life was typical middle-class, fully and unconditionally loved by parents, grandparents, aunts, uncles, and cousins. My father worked as a computer programmer at Dow Jones, and my mother was a student at Rider College. My grandparents lived next to us on a tree-lined street facing the local high school. My siblings and I attended private school. It was a family tradition to gather at my grandparent's home Friday evenings to enjoy crispy fried fish and steamed crabs. At some point during one of these gatherings, my mother must have shared with my grandmother about me losing my hair because I was quickly wedged between my grandmother's knees, getting my tender scalp dabbed with cotton balls dampened with bleach that did not work. "This looks like ringworm," She said with confidence. More spots kept appearing until my scalp could be seen through the few sparse hairs that remained.

Finally, my mother took me to see a dermatologist. Dr. Goldman diagnosed me with alopecia areata at the age of eight. Immediately, my treatment started using Ultraviolet light therapy, creams, and eventually steroid injections into my scalp. Ultimately, the steroid injections proved to be the most effective. My hair grew back, and we thought we were done with Alopecia; little did we know that this disease would be a part of me forever.

Luckily, I don't remember being bullied or made fun of in elementary school. Alopecia was just something that I had, and fortunately, my mother could do a mean comb-over. I would think Alopecia would have made me somewhat of a shrinking violet during high school, but it didn't. I was a cheerleader throughout high school and even served as captain of my squad. I remember one day being called baldie by one of the basketball players, and yes, it did hurt my feelings, but I suffered that in silence. It did not occur to me to shy away from cheering my school's team to a championship. Even the name-calling knucklehead received my genuine, good-natured team spirit. Go Cougars!

I think menopause has had a great deal to do with my alopecia areata progressing to alopecia universalis at fifty-seven. Alopecia universalis is, as the name implies, total hair loss all over the body. The hardest part of this new diagnosis is wrapping my mind around the fact that my hair may never grow back. Now, one might ask, "No shaving or bikini waxes?" Sounds like a positive takeaway from this negative drama, but what I wouldn't give to have razors on my shopping list.

A turning point happened while I was shopping for a dress for an event. I must have tried on a dozen outfits, and nothing was working. I slumped onto the fitting room bench, crying because my reflection was pitiful, and I felt so hopeless and unattractive. The truth was that nothing in the entire store would have made me feel attractive. My true beauty would come from an inner confidence I would soon discover. I had adopted the habit of covering my head with a cotton cap and never left home without it. As I slid the cap from my head, I had an epiphany. The thought occurred to me that I would have to find a way to accept this new hairlessness. My reflection still taunted me. *What's the use you are still bald?* I shook the thought from my mind. This was not going to be me. I had to find a way to embrace and accept what would not go away overnight. I still had some sexy left in here somewhere. I felt like Sandy from the movie Grease as I left the store in search of something that would turn this miserable ship around.

The morning of my event, I went to the beauty supply store looking for nail polish and inspiration for what to do about my head. God ordered my steps because I noticed packets of colorful tattoos of birds, flowers, and other metallic designs hanging on metal rods at the checkout counter. I thought, *why not*? It would be something different. I remember seeing a young girl on Instagram who suffered from Alopecia going to her senior prom. Her mother was an artist and painted beautiful flowers on her daughter's bald head. I thought the look was stunning. So, right there on Martin Luther King Drive in Southwest Atlanta, I believed I'd found my answer. After I showered, dressed, and applied my makeup to perfection, I retrieved the plastic bag that contained the tattoos. I had no idea how this would turn out, but something within kept nudging me forward. I purchased three gold metallic tattoos. I applied one tattoo down the back center of my head and one on the side. I forgot to trim the tattoo and unknowingly adhered the barcode to my scalp (trial and error). But my husband helped me to remove the barcode with alcohol, being very careful not to touch the gold tattoo design. I wore white, cropped jeans and a white swing shirt and hot red lipstick.

I walked into Mr. Gregory Porter's concert like I was about to take the stage. I felt so emboldened. I felt the stares and heard the whispers. I don't know what was said, and I didn't care; it felt so good not to hide under a hat. As I was taking my seat, I realized that my choice, albeit not for everyone, was a liberating one for me. And I would later learn the impact it would have on women, men, and children of all ethnic backgrounds. So many people stopped me daily with, "Sis, your head is beautiful, love the tattoos! You got me thinking about shaving my head!" I was thinking, *darn, here I am, worried about what Alopecia took from me, and people think I opted to shave my head and wear the colorful tattoos as a personal choice.* A young woman complimented me on the beautiful tattooed design, and I responded with my usual, "Thank you." She, in turn, replied, "No, thank you."

Living with Alopecia has taught me many lessons. One is adapting to adversity, to accept and give myself some grace. Two, how to walk into a room and own it. And three, everybody has something, seen and unseen; the difference is how we choose to deal with our issues. We must face, study, and use them to make ourselves stronger and better for the journey. There are several support groups for those suffering from Alopecia. The National Alopecia Areata Foundation (NAAF) is a supportive and encouraging group. Find your village, people who love and care about you, and lean on them when you need to.

Alopecia can be a devastating disease, but as I put things into perspective, things could be much worse. I must thank God for my portion. These days, I may be in public without a tattoo or cap in sight. I have realized on my journey that I must be okay with myself. Would I love to have a full head of hair? Yes, I certainly would. I miss my hair. But the lessons I have learned about myself are invaluable. The last important lesson I gained is the confidence to walk into any room and know I am enough, shiny bald head and all!

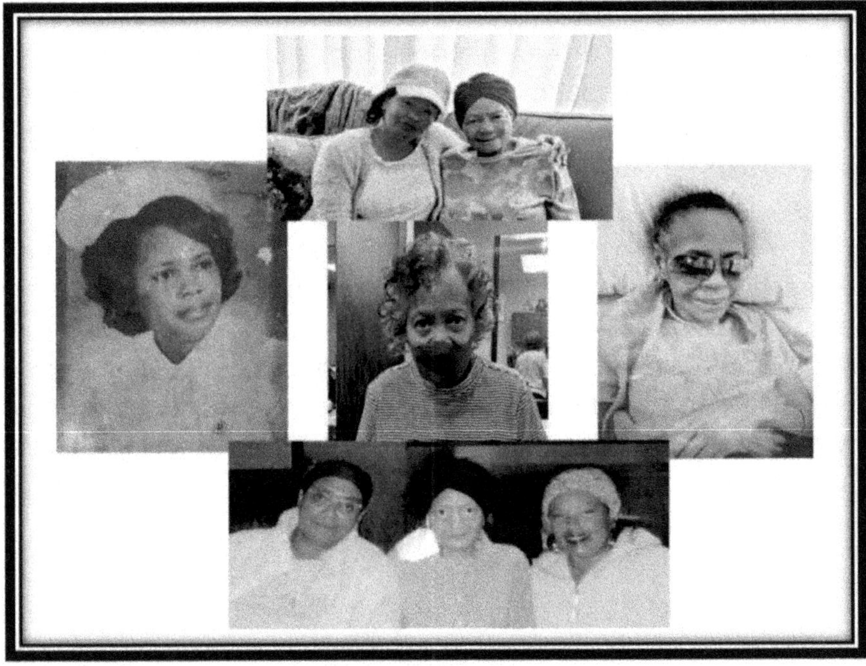

Beatrice and Her Sisters

A Calling to Caregiving and Sisterhood
By Beatrice Hunter Pack

About 1 in 3 adults in the United States provides care to other adults as informal caregivers. ~ Mayo Clinic.

I am the sixth child of nine siblings. My sister Cathy is the oldest, born in the 1940s. After her birth, my parents migrated from Florida to New York in search of greater opportunities, escaping the cruel hardships of picking hundreds of pounds of cotton for a pittance.

In our home, a good work ethic was paramount. Dad (Estell) owned and managed a dry cleaner but loved tinkling with vintage automobiles. Mom (Beatrice) worked various jobs until the responsibilities of having nine children compelled her to devote most of her time to parenting and grandparenting. She was affectionally called Big Ma by her grandchildren. Later, she was called to ministry and her favorite reply to how are you was- "I'm fine in the Lord, pressing on in Jesus' name" Mom preached the significance of family and compassion, constantly admonishing us to "watch out for one another." Her motherly advice and pastoral lessons greatly influenced my life and caregiving path.

My sister Cathy was fifteen years my senior.

She had brilliant, piercing eyes, thick lips, and a deep-set dimple in her chin. Like my mother, she was lovely. Cathy worked as a nurse in two nursing homes for forty-five years. From our discussions about her work and patients, I knew Cathy took her position very seriously and cared deeply about her patients.

Cathy was previously married and had three sons. She was a devoted mother and a great cook. I can still smell the aroma of her collard greens, they were delicious and one of my favorite dishes of hers. Her kitchen table was an enjoyable place. She would invite friends and family members over to break bread, and we shared many great stories and precious memories.

Her son, TJ, was kind. His smile was contagious, and his spirit was adventurous. They were very close. Even when TJ became ill and died, she handled it with the abiding grace of a Christian woman. Cathy was a deeply spiritual woman.

Her faith was unwavering; she laid him to rest in a spirit of peace and calm despite the pain only a mother could feel.

The death of a child is an experience that is hard to fathom for a parent, but Cathy's belief in God was anchored in grace, and it sustained her. I felt that Cathy and I stood in harmony the day she buried her son, trading fear for love.

Cathy's relationship with God grew as she became an evangelist and worked tirelessly to share the gospel's good news. Her love for people showed in how she cared for her family, patients, and friends.

After TJ's death, she developed a deeper relationship with his son. Later, her grandson moved into her home. She guided him into adulthood, and they shared a decade of love.

Several years after retirement, Cathy's body began to reap the effects of aging. She fell and broke her back, ripping her from the comforts of a home. She worked tirelessly to build, to being placed into a health care facility. Suddenly, her career in nursing and caring for others reversed. She was no longer a caregiver; she had become the patient. Her health continued to decline, and her stay went from days to weeks, then months to years, from rehabilitation to long-term care. She was trapped in a hopeless system, now stripped of her independence. Her sons and grandchildren could not provide the care her aging and sickness demanded. Upon hearing about her trauma, I was drawn to a place of loving-kindness and compassion for my oldest sister and wanted to help her, so we planned a visit to

New York. I visited the nursing home with my sisters, Loretta and Trish, to encourage Cathy. She looked weak, like starvation had set in, her hair grayed and pulled back with skin so pale it appeared ghostly. I was afraid because, at that time, Cathy was in hospice. We prayed, told her we loved her and finished with humor in hopes of encouraging her. Before our visit ended, she smiled and said, "Thank you for traveling here to see me." I sensed a spark of hope ignite that day, rooted in sisterhood; Cathy mattered, and our presence solidified it.

After that visit, my compassion grew, and I found it unjust for her to transition from this life without steadfast advocacy in her care planning. Also, Loretta reflected on how she blessed her life with order and kindness, so we agreed to become her caregivers. We established an action plan and routinely visited with Cathy and the social workers in New York. During our visits, we discovered many obstacles; Cathy was diagnosed with a debilitating disease, many financial stressors, while locked in a problematic system that was only effective with consistent advocacy, frequent visitors, and our belief in the power of prayer. Our sister wanted to move to Michigan with us after her health improved from hospice to long-term care. After years of discussions with the nursing home on how the relocation process worked, they called and were ready to assist us with her request to relocate. Moving patients out of state is a complex process. It would be best to have dedicated teams within the nursing home system and family to drive the process to completion. Now, the facility was motivated because it was closing due to hardships from the Pandemic and needed to place patients expeditiously. Cathy's prayers to relocate were finally answered. I was retired, and Loretta had flexibility with her employer. Together, we began the process of establishing our sister's residency. Loretta would give care at night, and I took the day shift. No matter how well prepared we thought we were, something came up lacking – like the need for new specialists, additional doctors, insurance updates, education on dementia, and a plethora of unexpected medical and administrative needs. We also had to renegotiate family participation as things changed. I gave myself grace as often as needed and found peace with being human. My husband agreed to help during Cathy's move, allowing me the flexibility required for business appointments. Over a year later, she suffered a stroke in my arms at home. I remember yelling out her name from the pit of my soul. My husband ran into the bathroom to help pull her limp body up. My heart and mind raced with fear, and I asked God, *"Please do not let her die on my watch – not on my watch, Lord."*

I was too familiar with the piercing pain felt from losing a loved one and the nagging question: Did you do everything possible? In addition to the backdraft from the quiet critics. So, I prayed for more time and grace. Within moments, Cathy's eyes opened. She looked bewildered as we sat her down. Emergency Medical Service/EMS arrived. They examined her, took her vitals, asked questions, and said she appeared okay, so they left. However, I still felt unsure, and she was still foggy. I called Loretta. After our discussion, I decided to take Cathy to the hospital's emergency unit; they confirmed she suffered a stroke.

Caregiving was taking its toll on us. There was little time to take care of myself or household responsibilities. I was still recovering from an injury and in pain.

So, I was admitted to the hospital as a patient with Cathy. Now, I could advocate for her because she had dementia and needed help communicating her symptoms. It gained Cathy valuable treatment time. The doctors established the critical window for emergency treatment after a stroke is up to 3- 4.5 hours, followed by intensive rehabilitation to yield the best results. A week later, my sister was discharged and doing much better, and I was rested and ready to start again. Caregiving is a labor of love; at times, I was overcome with joy that I was making a positive difference in the life of someone I loved. Other times, I was overwhelmed with guilt, questioning whether I was doing enough because I missed serving a meal that day or made a medical decision, then second-guessing myself. Thank God for my sister Loretta. She was my partner and sounding board; we tackled caregiving together and found solace in each other.

Also, my husband and children were a great help when I needed a time-out for self-care. It takes an enduring support system to lessen the disruption of caregiving. I believe being a caregiver is a gift from God, even when balancing everything is tough. It is challenging to juggle the increased needs of a loved one. Yet, I found personal growth and a new purpose in supporting my sister, which helped me balance the stress and difficulties of the caregiver journey. I grew more aware of seniors' disparity in insurance costs, prescription drugs, and health care needs. That is why I decided to advocate for change, and I urge you to contact your state representatives and let them know you care about these issues. I searched online and listed a couple of resources we used- AARP, which advocates for quality of life as we age, and Medicare.gov, which provides a tool that rates the quality of nursing homes by State. The caregiving journey gave me clarity on aging; aging is an inevitable part of life, and we can start doing things to enhance the aging process. I developed a mindset of gratitude and started a healthier lifestyle around food. Patience became my friend, especially when Cathy asked me the same question for the eighth time. Now, we laugh with acceptance and love during those times. We continue to weather the storms of life and adjust the caregiver/patient relationship; it is easier now because we are wiser and more tolerant. The calling of caregiving and sisterhood brought the three of us together and our faith gave us the courage to do what needed to be done. I am so grateful for my foundation of faith built on grace, love and mercy- strong enough to anchor me during the stressors of caregiving until we begin experiencing the joy of just being sisters again.

Surprisingly, life has a way of centering us just before our breaking points. After the stroke, Cathy needed rehabilitation and continuous medical care. Therefore, we began the search for the best facility. Today, Cathy thrives peacefully in an established long-term care nursing home that uses strategies like the Eden Alternative concept, caring for spirit and body. Nine months after the stroke, our sister is 82 years old and thriving. She is a survivor and continuously expresses her gratitude to us. We visit her frequently, take her out to eat, sing, and laugh with her, and on excellent days, she remembers and shares family stories as we count our blessings in gratitude for our sisterhood founded on love.

In Matthew 14:32-33 (KJV), Jesus commanded the storm to be still. Today, God's grace is still sufficient in our troubles. I know Him to be a very present help in my times of need. He calms and restores me. May you find grace in your many endeavors, especially the gift of caregiving and sisterhood.

Loving Wisdom
A Second Collection of Stories That Nourish the Soul

The End
By Joan Wagnon Drescher

We come across *the end* in lots of different scenarios. It is a fairy tale we read to our children: It's the end of a beautiful day with a magnificent sunset, a relationship, and a job, to name a few. My end refers to my life. The end will come for all of us. It's not something we can avoid and is inevitable. To lose a family member is a difficult experience. The process is akin to nothing we go through, no matter the circumstances. We all know death will come, but that doesn't soften the blow. I hope everyone reading this will be open to exploring this difficult topic in new and open ways.

Recently, my husband's stepmother was in the throes of dying. Witnessing her health decline was terrible; Losing her independence and consequent helplessness were debilitating for all involved. So many loved her: a husband, two daughters, stepchildren, a sister, me, a stepdaughter-in-law, extended family, and friends all stood by and watched as our hearts broke in disbelief. How could this be? She was a vibrant, healthy, funny, loving, and wonderful person but was now forced to succumb to a failing and dying body full of cancer. Within a couple of months, our loved one was gone, but our last memories would not be the ones we cherished.

We are still numb, trying to process and accept her loss as we process it in different ways. I am witnessing my family coping. We have accepted that she is gone, and we are now grieving. I understand allowing ourselves to grieve, heal from our pain and loss, and remember our loved one in positive, loving, and joyful ways is important. This is a process that takes time and is unique to each individual.

A few years ago, I watched my mother slowly decline in mental and physical capabilities. The process took many years. She was diagnosed with Alzheimer's and was slowly stripped of her ability to reason and function. Watching this once independent and wonderful person slowly decline was a tragic thing to experience.

I joined an Alzheimer's Support Group to better understand my mother. I wanted to understand what she was going through and how I could best help her. It was sobering listening to the others in the group. Each person's experience and situation were different, but at the same time, there were many similarities. There were suggestions for what to say and what not to say to someone with dementia. Don't ask too many questions. Don't challenge or correct them. If they think they are living in the past, go with it. Be patient. Don't take it personally if they are mean or accusatory of certain things. The list was long, and the role of the caregiver or loved one was difficult.

As a result of these experiences, I have concluded that my death is something I want to face and plan. Needless trauma and heartache for those left behind is something I don't want for my family. As a healthy sixty-something individual, I'm doing this now so I can be at peace and continue to live a full life and not worry about my end. I'll be comfortable knowing that my husband and children will not be faced with watching my decline. I do not want my husband to have to become my caregiver. As importantly, I would not ask this of my children. For these reasons, I have chosen what I see as a better option for us all.

I'm sure others find themselves in similar situations as witnesses to the tragic loss of a loved one. To be so close to this was a true eye-opener for me. Why should anyone have to endure such pain and suffering? Also, why should family and friends have to witness and experience this happening?

Can't there be a better ending for what was a vibrant, happy, and fulfilling life? The answer I came to is yes. There can be a different end. I began researching and educating myself so I could have a better understanding and insight into these issues. The conclusion I came to is that I don't want the final curtain call I just witnessed. I hope to go out in a way that suits who I am and what I want. I'm calling this "the gift." It will be a gift for my family and those who loved me.

I realize that many events might take place that could alter what I envision will happen. Life can present many unknowns, twists and turns, and events we cannot predict or even imagine. If something unexpected or sudden happens to me and my plan does not go into effect, that's okay. I aim to make my wishes known and help guide my loved ones. An attorney will help me write a directive to spell out how I want my life's final months and days to play out.

Unfortunately, due to the current prohibitive legislation in the United States, it is difficult to receive an assisted suicide. Dignitas is a non-profit member society founded in 1998 located in Switzerland. "To live with dignity - To die with dignity" is their doctrine. This is where I wish to go. Of course, they have a strict protocol that must be followed, and I hope I will meet their criteria when my end of life arrives. I desire my husband to be by my side. For me, this has been an empowering decision. I realize a lot of people may not agree. I understand, and that's fine. We must each respect what others choose for themselves and their decisions regarding their death.

Again, losing a loved one is difficult, no matter the circumstances or how prepared we may think we are for that loss. We have the right to make our own decisions regarding our lives. We should expect this same right as to the decisions regarding our death. I am choosing to script my End. Hopefully, this gift will help my loved ones avoid the pain and suffering we had to witness my husband's stepmother and my mother endure. Everyone deserves to live with dignity and to die with dignity.

Grace and Mercy
By La Verne C. Dixon

The Birth

I was born on March 6, 1948, and died on June 14, 1978. I died again on March 4, 2023.

The circumstances of my birth were an early indication of the peculiar life I would lead. My mama was alone when she went into premature labor. She was a nurse, and I was her second child, so she was not particularly alarmed. Then, suddenly, feeling uncomfortable escalated into excruciating pain. This change paralyzed all of her bravado. She didn't have a telephone, so she called on the name of Jesus. Miraculously, my Uncle Homer appeared at the door. He bundled her into his car, intending to take her to the County Hospital.

Mama told him the baby was coming, and she couldn't stop it. They were miles away from County Hospital, where Blacks were allowed to be treated. Hillside Hospital, the all-white hospital, was less than a mile away, so that's where they went. They made it as far as the elevator. I entered this world in the elevator, and my mama did not know whether she would be accepted or thrown out. So Mama did what she knew to do. She prayed. I was born so fast that it caused my head to be deformed. Mercifully, when the elevator came to a stop, Mama's screams brought help. Mama said the doctors went to work immediately. They feverishly molded my skull into something recognizable. I was the first Black child born in Hillside Hospital. They took excellent care of us. They were so proud of themselves that they hung my little chocolate picture in the lobby, which stayed until they tore down the building.

The Awakening

I married my husband during the height of the Vietnam War. I was pregnant with our first child when he got the call to serve and was immediately deployed to that war-torn hell. He had no say in the matter. Back then, Uncle Sam ordered you to go, and you went. I had a difficult pregnancy. Then, in my sixth month, I was involved in a terrible car accident. I spent the rest of my pregnancy in an all-white, Orange County, California hospital. There were no other Black patients or employees. I was blissfully ignorant of the issue of my Blackness.

The Black population in San Diego at that time was about 3%. There were no Black radio stations and no Black television programs. The only Black people on television were maids and buffoons. The only Black-owned businesses were BBQ hole-in-the-wall restaurants and beauty and barber shops. If I looked hard enough, I could find a Black record store where I could buy our music. We were politely segregated. I was not aware of the civil rights struggle. I had never heard of Martin Luther King, Andrew Young, or John Lewis.

The hospital in Orange County was close to Los Angeles, and the news programs were more diverse than I had ever seen. I began to be aware of the civil rights struggle. But I was very ignorant as to the pertinence of the movement. I did not put together what it had to do with me. I was just fascinated by all those Black people on television.

One day, my respiratory therapist, who was Hawaiian, came to see me, but it wasn't time for my therapy. He looked uncomfortable. My immediate concern was for my baby. He told me he was so sorry for my loss. Then I panicked. I thought for sure my husband had been injured or killed in action. He said he was chosen to relate some bad news because he was the closest thing to being Black. That's when he told me Martin Luther King Jr. had been assassinated. They didn't know that I barely knew who he was, nor his significance or what he should have meant to me.

The months wore on, and I was still hospitalized. I needed to prepare for the birth of my baby. I had no family nearby, and my husband was still in Vietnam. My roommate and other military wives got together and gave me a baby shower, but I had to convince my doctor to let me go. He only gave me a temporary discharge if I agreed to check myself back into the hospital after the shower. Everything was beautiful. I was given everything I needed, including a crib. When I stood to thank everyone for their generosity, my water broke. What followed was 16 hours of unimaginable pain. I was not prepared for the ferocity of childbirth. I had never heard of the many ways my body was exposed and violated. When I was finally given something to block the pain, it was useless. Then, it was time. Giving birth was like a science fiction movie. They put a mirror in front of me so I could watch the birth. I had no interest whatsoever in watching this horror. When my son entered the world, I held my breath until I heard his cry. Then, I turned my attention back to the horror in the mirror. I screamed at the image that was in front of me.

My son was the most beautiful baby I had ever seen. He had a head full of thick, long, silky curls the same color as peanut butter. His skin was a mixture of my Cherokee Indian and Creole and my husband's Sioux Indian and Black heritage. His eyes were large and dreamy, the same color as his hair., and he had long, beautiful eyelashes. He was also amazingly, alarmingly intelligent. We named him Roland Lorenzo Jr. and called him Little Roland.

I was surprised but grateful that he was alive. I had this feeling the entire time I carried him that my son would not live. He was premature and weighed only four pounds. We stayed in the hospital for three weeks. And when we were released, I was unprepared for the changes in my life. I was always sleep-deprived and tired, and I did not feel well. My son would abruptly wake up screaming all hours of the day and night. Then I hemorrhaged; unlike during childbirth, I passed sixteen blood clots the size of medium apples. I probably waited too long before I called for help, but I thought it would stop. I was nearly unconscious when the paramedics arrived. I had no one to take care of my baby, so they wrapped him up and put him in the ambulance with me. They put a bassinet in my hospital room so I could be close to him. To this day, I don't understand what happened to me. But we survived.

The Betrayal

Four months later, Little Roland still woke up at random times screaming. I often took him to the doctor, concerned that he might be in pain. He was such a sweet, affectionate old soul. My heart broke every time he cried. I knew something was wrong despite what the doctors said. He was the love of my life and my heart and soul. I had fought hard to keep him safe in and out of my womb.

Of equal concern was that the husband who went to Vietnam and the husband who returned home were not the same. The only time he seemed at peace was when he held his son. We moved from Orange County to Long Beach near his station. As soon as we moved, I made an appointment with the pediatrician at the VA hospital. Someone finally listened to me and did a complete work-up on Little Roland. When we were called in for the results, I was hopeful we would finally have an answer; however, I didn't get the answer I hoped for. The doctor showed us an x-ray of our baby's heart. His heart covered his entire chest cavity. I fought to breathe. The doctor called St. Mary's Hospital in Long Beach and arranged for our son to be admitted. After examining him, they told us he would need a heart catheterization. I had brought our son into the hospital for a routine check-up, and now I was leaving without him. When I got home, I stood in the middle of his room. My arms felt so empty.

We were allowed to visit him before the procedure. He was screaming and was in so much pain. I could not comfort him because of the need for a sterile environment. We were not allowed to hold him. After his procedure, we were told that he had a hole in his heart, and if they did not attempt to repair it, he could die the next time he cried. We were also told that he might not survive the surgery. They urged us to visit with him for perhaps the last time. My husband was in complete denial, and so I went alone. I stood by the incubator and watched my child with full knowledge of the extent of his suffering. The glass box feeding him oxygen would not allow me to touch him. I wanted to run my fingers through his beautiful curls and wipe away his tears. I wanted to kiss his little peanut butter cheeks and whisper that everything would be okay. But I knew deep within my soul that this was the last time I would see him alive. I wanted to hold my baby. Oh, how I wanted to hold my baby.

When they took him away, I suggested to my husband that we go home and return later. The surgery would take five to seven hours. We went home. I was so nervous and flustered that I cooked enough dinner for the rest of the week. I did the laundry and cleaned everything that had a speck of dust. I felt in my soul the moment my precious baby boy became an angel, and I knew I would be in no shape to do anything. When we returned to the hospital, we were met by the surgeon and invited to a small room. I whispered to my husband that it was bad. The doctor got straight to the point. Our son was gone.

I truly did not understand why God did this to me. I had served him my entire life. I grew up with my grandfather, who was a pastor, as my constant companion and absorbed his every teaching. At age eight, I decided to walk down the aisle at Bethel Baptist church to give my life to Christ. I, with no prodding, asked to be baptized. I, who, as a teen, spent more time in church than anywhere else. I did not understand.

The Crucifixion

I located a church nearby and began the long journey to healing. Both terrified and exhilarated, I told my pastor I was going to have another child. He provided invaluable support to us during that time.

My husband confided that he tried hard to give me another child so that I could finally stop crying. He wanted another son, but we had a beautiful peaches and cream little girl. I was so afraid something was going to happen to her. My husband insisted on naming her after me. We called her Red. Then we got the news that my husband was going back to Vietnam. My tiny princess was only four months old, the exact age of my son at the time of his death. My husband took the news to a whole other level. First, it was disbelief, then anger, and finally, total irrational fear. I promised him I would do something. I went to his commander and told him I needed my husband with me. I could not do this alone. In the Pentecostal church, I was taught that God rewards goodness with blessings and wreaks His wrath on those who commit sin. I believed that I had done wrong and God was punishing me. My pastor assured me that I was not a horrible sinner and God was a loving God. He said God was not punishing me.

So, I went to church that Sunday as usual. I needed to pray that the military would release my husband early. I loved God, but I did not know God for myself. I only knew God through the preacher. Whatever the preacher said, however, the preacher interpreted the Word of God was what I believed. I had not read the Bible from page one through the end. I thought all preachers were good, like my grandpa.

Five or six women stood on the doorstep when I got to the church. They moved in unison as I approached the door to block my entry. One by one, they hurled hideous insults at me. I was called a home wrecker and a whore. I was berated for bringing my bastard child to the church and throwing her into the face of the preacher's wife. It took my naïve mind a few minutes to figure out what they were alluding to. When it dawned on me, I was mortified. These women were wrong. I did not sleep with my pastor; my baby was not his child! In the first place, I didn't even swear or lie. I would rather roll over and play dead rather than hurt anyone. In the second place, preachers didn't do that sort of thing. That was adultery. That was a horrible sin.

Something came over me. I looked down at my sleeping child snuggled in my chest. Then I looked at the women. Without a word, I turned and walked away. I said, "Okay, God, I get it. You don't want me. You hate me. So, I hate you, too. I don't want you either." For ten long years, I was like Saul. I cursed God. I ridiculed anyone who believed in God. I called anyone who went to church a hypocrite because of my convoluted interpretation of sin. And I was empty. Dead on the inside.

Grace, Mercy, and Forgiveness

I had told my husband a thousand times not to place the lawn mower next to the hot water heater. I was doing laundry and had just put the clothes in the gas dryer and walked away. There was a loud boom, and a powerful force threw me down the hall. Smoke and flames were everywhere. Instinctively, I knew I had to get out of there somehow. I called on the name of the Lord. I whispered to the Lord to please help me. And more importantly, I knew that He would.

I heard a glass break, and someone shouted my name. Then I was outside in the fresh air. I watched the paramedics as they leaned over my still body and announced that I had no pulse and was not breathing. Before I could process what was happening, I was sucked into a tunnel with a white opening. I emerged on the bank of a beautiful river. Across the river, I heard voices singing. It was not just any old song, but perfect and in amazing harmony. They sang joyful praises to the Lord. The sky across the river was like the searchlights at the airport. Only the colors were gold and green and every color of the rainbow.

There was a presence with me that was indescribable. It felt like pure love. I realized It was the Lord. Oh, how I had missed His presence. He told me that I must go back. I said I did not want to. He told me to go back and tell His people they only had time to learn to love like him. When I awoke from my coma five days later, I didn't tell anyone anything. Years later, I came across an article about people who had experienced something similar to what I had experienced. It even had a name, Near Death Experiences. I worked for a well-known hospital supporting the families of the Missing and Murdered Children of Atlanta. I told George, our head psychologist, I had the same experience. He asked me to tell him all about it. The advice the psychologist gave me taught me how to live again.

The Resurrection

Forty-three years later, I finally obeyed the directive given to me by the Lord. November 11, 2022, I delivered the message. It was entitled "We Don't Have Time for This and That." I was now Rev. La Verne Dixon. Strangely, I felt that I would die after I delivered that message. Much older, I had health issues and experienced intermittent shortness of breath. The cardiologist and pulmonologist tests found no cause. So, I kept going. I loved my position as outreach minister and minister of pastoral care. My work just sort of evolved because of a need. I worked hard. I enjoyed my work.

Such a simple-sounding message from the Lord, but it took me forty-three years to truly comprehend it. I endured a lot of injustice. Many mistook my kindness for naivety and weakness. What was not understood was that it was my love and my kindness that gave me my strength. I learned that sharing my love should not depend on how the recipient of that love responds.

I noticed that some of the Deacons in the church seemed uneasy praying publicly; they needed instruction and encouragement to give them confidence. The Diaconate were planning their first retreat since the pandemic. I was scheduled to give a presentation on prayer, and I was excited. I stayed up very late because I love to write while the world is asleep. My youngest daughter was in the Army Reserves and was away that weekend. On my way to the church that morning, I got that old familiar premonition that someone would die. I usually don't know who it is, but I can tell by the severity of my pain how close that person is to me.

This time, I knew it was me. I had felt this coming for a little while. So, I prayed and asked the Lord for more time. I knew I had not yet fulfilled my mission on this earth. But I also knew something was holding me back and that something needed to move. So I prayed and asked God to heal my body and give me what I needed. I was a little tired that day but otherwise felt fine. We had a delicious breakfast with lots of conversation. It was wonderful to be in fellowship once again. I was almost finished with my presentation when I became short of breath. I rushed through to the end, determined to finish. Then, I began to cough a little. Now, I am a person who does not easily say I need help. However, I turned to the person beside me and told them, "I think you need to call 911." Then, I moved towards the rear of the building to avoid disturbing the next presentation. The person sitting next to me had a similar, less severe experience. He followed me when I left. There was a doctor present and a registered nurse. The doctor said it was like an out-of-body experience. She said she doesn't even remember moving. But she did move and began chest compressions. She also said that she started not to come that day, but she did. She functioned that day as an angel. The ambulance arrived in seven minutes. The EMT team said the first people they encountered were in a circle of prayer. They prayed hard. They prayed fervently from their souls. I had taught them to pray from their heart. The second angel took over the chest compressions, and although my heart had stopped, she kept going. Briefly, I regained a heartbeat, but then it stopped again. By now, we were at the hospital. The medical team did not give up until they brought me back. God moved everyone around that day like the Master Coordinator that He is. In retrospect, I was surrounded by angels.

From what I have been told, my last words were that I would be back. The next thing I remember was a bright light. It looked like a spaceship. Then, as I became more aware, I realized they were people. Not just any people but my family who had transitioned to life Everlasting. I concentrated on the one I missed the most: my mama. They smiled and waved goodbye as they receded into the heavens. I knew immediately what had happened. I also knew that I would be just fine. I jokingly thought that God didn't have to go that far, but I bet everyone knew how to pray now. After I learned more about what happened, I could process it. Make no mistake about it: God took me away, and He set everything in place to bring me back.

Love, Purpose, and Peace

A lot has changed. A young man was present as the professionals worked to restore my heart. He was deeply touched. When he sees me now, he looks at me lovingly and hugs me. The Diaconate has a new commitment to serve. Faith was increased, and understanding was gained. God's amazing grace was manifested to those who witnessed my death and resurrection. We were all blessed to be in the presence of the true and Living God. He touched each one of us for His purposes.

I do have survivor's trepidation, more apprehension than outright fear. Not for me, but for others. Why can't we know God the way He wants us to know Him instead of how we want to know Him?

I am different now. In a way that I cannot explain. I know that many people love me, and I am so thankful. I remember one day, I wondered who would be at my funeral. Would I be appreciated? I don't want an obituary outlining my degrees and awards and what someone thinks I accomplished in this life. That's like blowing in the wind. Only what I do for the Lord matters to Him and me. I want to be known for my love. I want to live by the wisdom of King Solomon, who reminded us *it is only what we do for the Lord that matters.*

The doctors still cannot agree on what caused my heart failure for seventeen minutes. Or how my aorta is bleeding just right. They are flabbergasted with how quickly my ribs healed and why I have all my faculties. They don't understand how I only spent two weeks in the hospital with just a few days in ICU.

I understand. Like the Apostle Paul said, "At first, I understood in part, but now I fully understand."

Caregiving, Covid, And Constant Inner Criticism
Bouncing Back When Life Has You On The Ropes
By Malena Cunningham Anderson

I was an adventurous, confident, and curious child. I talked a lot and asked a lot of questions. I loved traveling, reading, talking back, and taking risks. I couldn't wait to leave my small town in South Carolina to attend the University of Georgia, where I graduated early and moved to the big city of Atlanta. I had a fabulous career in journalism, where I secured plum jobs in several states as a news reporter and anchor. I traveled the world, befriended famous people, and produced award-winning documentaries. Later in life, I married a great guy. It appeared that my life was a dream until 2017.

I never knew how strong I was until being strong was my only choice.

Christmas Day, 2017

The day after my husband and I spent time with family in South Carolina, I called home to wish Mother Merry Christmas. When she answered, she sounded so weak that it frightened me. She told me she'd been in bed all day. When I asked where my brother and niece, who lived with her, were, she said they were out celebrating. Mother had not eaten anything or taken any medicine. She had no idea when anyone would return home, so I called a cousin to check in on Mother. After she arrived, my cousin suggested I rush home the next day. I did. I found my mother weaker and almost delirious. I rushed Mother to the emergency room, where she was admitted to the hospital a few hours later. A series of doctors came to her room to deliver test results. Mother had pneumonia, an aneurysm in her stomach, and complete kidney failure. I was stunned and afraid. At 82 years old, I questioned how she could survive all these health challenges simultaneously. One doctor suggested I prepare for what could be the worst possible outcome. I refused.

Instead, I went downstairs to the hospital chapel to talk with God. I returned to my past and recalled how my grandmothers, aunts, and other female elders were examples of walking in faith. Now more than ever was the time to rely on all the lessons I had learned from Sunday school, summer church revivals, and family prayers. My conversation went something like this:

"Lord, I'm not ready for you to take my mother yet. But not my will but, thy will be done. If you let her survive this, I will do everything in my power to care for my mother in these golden sunset years. I just ask that you give me the strength to prepare for what I can't possibly know or see that is to come."

I spent two weeks in my mother's room, consulting with various doctors. Among them, a kidney specialist and a vascular surgeon informed me of the road ahead for my mother's health. It was touch and go, and it wouldn't be easy. Thanks to prayer, my mother pulled through. Remarkably, she barely remembered anything from those two weeks in the hospital.

Afterward came four weeks of rehab and a lifetime of dialysis. For me, that meant weekly trips traveling I-85 to and from Atlanta to Greenville, SC, to care for her and help maintain her household and financial affairs, crying on most trips. One day, while in South Carolina, I was overwhelmed by all that was happening and decided to go for a drive to clear my head. During the ride, I cried and sang along with the gospel songs on the radio. To my surprise, I saw a sign that said, "Welcome to Tennessee!" I thought, *how in the world did I drive to Tennessee*? I was oblivious to the time or location. I quickly turned around and made the three-hour drive back to Greenville.

After a year of this, my husband became concerned for my sanity and safety on the road. He sat down with me and my mother to ask her to consider moving to Atlanta with us. We believed it would be the best arrangement. Mother agreed to the move, and things changed again in less than a year. We were on lockdown because of the COVID-19 pandemic. Life as I knew it had changed drastically, and it would only get even more challenging from there.

My husband, an attorney, was forced to close his office in a downtown Atlanta high-rise and work from home. Mother still had dialysis three days a week and numerous monthly doctor appointments. COVID or not, she still needed life-saving services that could only be delivered away from our home. We were always mindful, secluded, and careful in those months without a vaccine. The virus showed little mercy on the elderly, infirmed, and obese. I prayed my mother, who had no choice but to leave the house, would not catch anything from the strangers she encountered at the dialysis clinic.

As the weeks and months of the pandemic continued, I grew weary and depressed being confined and semi-secluded. I had questions: When would there be a vaccine? How long before it was safe? When would life as we knew it return? Things I took for granted, like traveling, attending church, shopping, or eating out, were non-existent. I was surrounded 24-7 by my mother and husband; being all things to everyone tried my patience and physical, emotional, and mental health.

I've been a positive, happy, inquisitive person all my life. During the COVID years, I no longer recognized myself. I gained weight, barely combed my hair, and never wore makeup. I was intolerant and almost always in a bad mood. I started to feel pain all over my back, shoulders, and joints. It was as if my body aged overnight without warning. Oh, and those never-ending thoughts were constant replay. They were negative, nagging, and unrelenting thoughts of *why me, who am I, I didn't ask for this, why is this happening,* and *when will it end?* All played a never-ending loop inside my brain, and the torment lasted for months.

Then, one day, I was in my backyard and asked God to show me a sign. I wanted to know what my purpose was in life. Was it to simply be a wife and caregiver? If so, I needed God's help to accept those roles gracefully and peacefully. My calling as a content creator wasn't over, but it sure felt like it. I wanted no; I needed things to change. During the two-plus years of shutdown, I began to speak daily affirmations. I would take walks through the neighborhood and focus on nature, the plants, trees, deer, birds, and the weather. I was delighted to experience a newfound freedom and gratitude during these times. Suddenly, my motto became, *"Never take for granted what others wish they had."* I'd come home from these moments of meditation and was grateful to still have my 89-year-old mother with me. I was even more grateful to be married to a man who, during the pandemic, said little during my mood swings and outbursts. I was so thankful that he supported me in everything I tried to do to find peace.

Today, I'm in a better place. I believe that the pandemic was God's way of creating a time and a place to sit down and appreciate the life of blessings He had given me. Trust me, I continue to count them! In my quiet time, I was able to release so many of my negative thoughts, and with that release came an amazing release of pain in my body. I've also found a new outlet for my gifts and talents as an actor. In this new space, I can call up many of my life's challenges and experiences to help give depth to the characters I've been cast to play. I realize that my entire life's journey was in preparation for accepting and embracing my newfound peace, and for this, I am genuinely thankful to God.

A Closing Reflection
By Frances Johnson Dunston

In *Loving Wisdom, a Second Collection of Stories that Nourish the Soul,* the Wisdom Whisperers have shared their personal, intimate stories of life-defining challenges, tragedies, endurance, and resilience. They invite us into their inner sanctum to witness their unique journeys. With the power of their stories, they allow us to experience their unforeseen crises and to share the depths of their pain and sorrow, the indignities they suffer, and the burdens they are forced to bear. We observe how they come to terms with their adversities and challenges and learn to surmount them in victory. As we traverse their paths, we are led to a place of peace and understanding.

Through their stories, we learn that they endured their unexpected reckonings by drawing upon values instilled by family and ancestors early in life. We witness their faith in God, which gave them unfaltering assurance through their tribulations. We see the unwavering support of friends and loved ones who helped to carry them through the darkness into the light.

Their testimonies of perseverance teach us the ways and means by which we can meet our inevitable challenges along life's journey. They affirm our steadfast belief that we are similarly endowed to make our way, with the help of others, to enjoy the full measure of what living can bestow.

Thank you, Wisdom Whisperers, for the enlightenment and reassurance of each rendering.

More Of *Loving Wisdom* Is In The Making

We could not have anticipated the reciprocal rejoicing to be realized through putting our thoughts, reflections, and life experiences into print for others. Our diversity and common bonds as women make our words relatable and cause them to resonate with readers wherever we go. There is more we must share with you. The next anthology will be a collection of letters written from a contrasting philosophical perspective. It is not what we believe but that we believe in some higher power that gives richness to our whispers. Here is a preview of what lies in store in ***Loving Wisdom, A Collection of Inspirational Letters***:

Greetings,

Let me formally introduce myself. I am your inner voice. My purpose is to comfort, lead, and guide you into all truth. God the Father calls me the "Holy Spirit. I have been waiting for the perfect time to speak to you, but you are busy. You are pulled in so many directions, and there is too much noise around you. Your life is filled with many distractions: work, family, church, committees, clubs, duties, financial obligations, to-do lists, goals, achievements, extracurricular activities, and social media. Not to mention the time and resources used to please people. I really need to talk to you! I have so much to share with you. But there's too much clutter in your life.

Every day, you wear so many hats. But you put on your security blanket when life is too much for you to bear or handle. You wear a mask. I can see that you are putting your guard up and are trying to protect your feelings. I'm not judging or trying to make you feel guilty. Believe me; this comes from a heart of love. So, please lower your defenses so you can truly hear me.

Do I have your undivided attention? Or will you be distracted by your emotions: fears, doubts, unbelief, brokenness, anxiety, loneliness, or depression? I must tell you, I've seen and felt it all as it happened to you. We are one. I have so much to share with you. I can't wait to shed light on your dark places. To finally stop you from obsessing with your failures and would have, could have flashbacks. You need to know that no weapon formed against you shall prosper (Isaiah 54:17), and greater is He that is in you than he that is in the world. (1 John 4:4) Do you really know *who you are* and *whose you are*?

Did you know God knew you before the foundation of the earth? Before there was time, you communed with God. That's right! You and God had a relationship. Because of this, you were thoughtfully and skillfully formed inside your mother's womb. You were given specific gifts and talents. You were not a mistake! God the Father spoke you into existence. (Jeremiah 1:5)

Your tears are so special that God has a very special bottle where He's kept them (Psalm 56:8). Your joys and pains, beginnings and endings, triumphs and failures, breakthroughs and setbacks are ever-present with the Lord. When you can't go on, He will carry you and give you a peace you can't understand (Philippians 4:7). You are constantly on His mind (Psalm 139:1-18).

Are you ready to let me take you beyond the surface and dive into your deepest thoughts, innermost feelings, greatest fears, and heart desires? Are you ready? Oh, I see, you're still not ready. You've been in this place so long that you've grown too familiar with it, and you can't see beyond your present condition. But know this: I'm not going anywhere. I am your inner voice, and we are one. I was there when you came to several crossroads, and you were prepared to meet the challenges, but for some reason, you or someone else made you feel like you could not do it. Remember, "You can do all things through Christ that strengthens you!" (Philippians 4:13). "You are more than a conqueror (Romans 8:37)." "Eyes have not seen, nor ears have heard all that God has in store for you (1 Corinthians 2:9)."

I hope I get a chance to speak to you again sooner than later because I have so much more to share with you. Please remember, I've seen it all and felt it all as if it was happening to you because *we are one*.

If your mind stays on Him, He will keep you in perfect peace (Isaiah 26:3).

Sincerely,
Inner Voice

By Mrs. Roberta Jackson

Read more of this letter and other missives by the Wisdom Whisperers in ***Loving Wisdom, A Collection of Inspirational Letters***.

Like a tree, a woman is life-giving, shade-yielding, and strong. When the winds of life are too strong and prove too harsh, a woman, just like a tree, will bend. But God. The stories so lovingly and heart-wrenchingly shared on the pages before you will take one's breath! Only the creator of a soul can balm that soul and set it upright to go forth and live on. These women, daughters, mothers, lovers, grandmothers, sisters, friends, and Whisperers not only live on but also thrive! Bent not broken, they continue to pour into their families and communities. Theirs are stories that, like the artists' tree, exhibit strength of heart! The Wisdom Whisperers are pictured beneath the Strength of Heart steel tree sculpture by artist Lynn Marshall-Linnemeier. This large steel sculptural tree is 18' high with two benches at its base and sits in the central portion of the Wolf Creek Library of the South Fulton, Georgia community.

Courage is the most important of all virtues because,
without courage, you can't practice any other virtue consistently.
You can practice any virtue erratically,
but nothing consistently without courage.
~ Maya Angelou

Wisdom Whisperers Shown: E. Paulette Smith-Epps, Rosalyn Roberts Mack, Lolita Browning Jackson, Joan Wagnon Drescher, Malena Cunningham Anderson, Gail Tusan Washington, Roberta Jackson, Tisa Jackson, Henrietta Stith Andrews, Joyce Coleman Edwards, La Verne Dixon.

Not pictured above: Leslie Hazle Bussey, Nina R. Hickson, Beatrice Hunter Pack, Frances Johnson Dunston.

The Wisdom Whisperers Biographies

Malena Cunningham Anderson

Malena Cunningham Anderson is a South Carolina native who graduated from the University of Georgia with a degree in journalism. Her career path led to her becoming a multiple Emmy Award-winning former news anchor and reporter who began her career working behind the scenes at CNN in Atlanta in 1982. She went on to work in several news markets in four states before retiring in 2004. Malena is also a documentary filmmaker and produced her first film, *Little Music Manchild*, which won the 2017 Best Documentary Award at Atlanta's BronzeLens Film Festival. Her second documentary, *SEED*, won the audience award at BronzeLens 2019. The COVID pandemic shut down documentary film production, and in 2021, Malena answered a casting call to do background work for a Showtime mini-series. A second background opportunity led to her getting picked up by TDH Talent Unlimited. Since signing with her agent, Malena has moved from the background to speaking roles in several television shows and commercials. In 2022, Malena was cast in a recurring role on the ALLBLK streaming series *Judge Me Not*. The show was written and produced by Judge Lynn Toler, of Divorce Court fame, and is loosely based on the judge's life. Also, in 2022, Malena booked a supporting lead role in a Lifetime movie, *Beware The Night Nurse*, which made its world debut on July 27, 2023. Malena is married to attorney Carl E. Anderson, II. She has two bonus children, five grandchildren, and two great-grandchildren.

Henrietta Stith Andrews

Henrietta Stith Andrews is a retired ordained minister with the United Church of Christ living in Powder Springs, Georgia. She graduated from Yankton College and earned a Master's in Early Childhood Education from Case Western Reserve University and a Master of Divinity from Lancaster Theological Seminary. In 2010, she completed the Dominican Center for Religious Development Graduate Program in Spiritual Direction. Henrietta is mother to Catherine and Stephen and grandmother to Elijah. A self-taught artist, poet, and author of My Short Hair Tells It All (2016), she delights in creating handmade quilts, abstract wall hangings, paper houses made of reused materials, and clothespin dolls.

Leslie Hazle Bussey

Leslie is CEO and Executive Director of GLISI, the Georgia Leadership Institute for School Improvement. She is a designer and curator of experiences that nourish the physical, social, psychological, and cognitive development of leaders and teams, understanding that the pathway to vibrant cultures of innovation in schools is not through knowing something different but by being and doing something different in how we interact with ourselves and each other. Her work developing leader soft skills includes developing the Resilience Circles experience for district and school leaders to navigate recovery from the 2020 pandemic, GLISI's framework of Six Leader SEL competencies, and GLISI's Leader SEL Toolkit. In addition to leading an agile and thriving nonprofit organization, Leslie enjoys cooking, yoga, and constantly learning new things just to communicate with her three children: Jordan (22), Ava (17), and Oliver (8).

La Verne C. Dixon

La Verne C. Dixon is an ordained minister who serves as Outreach Minister and Minister of Pastoral Care at First Congregational Church UCC, Atlanta. She also serves as Vice Moderator of the Southeast District of the United Church of Christ for the 2023-2024 conference year. She is a San Diego City College graduate majoring in English and Journalism, and she pursued additional studies at Point University with degrees in Human Relations with a minor in the Bible and the Preaching Ministries. In 1984, she was licensed and ordained in the African Methodist Episcopal Church, where she has been Pastor at five AME churches. In addition, La Verne's interest in the written word started at a young age and led to her first published work at eight. She ultimately launched her professional writing career with The San Diego Entertainment magazine. La Verne is passionate about helping other people. She generously gives her God-given gifts and talents as she listens, mentors, trains, and encourages others.

Joan Wagnon Drescher

Joan Drescher is a wife, mother, mother-in-law, and new grandmother! Her best and most rewarding job was raising her two children. She is the author of a children's book, *Penguins, Pizza, Peas, and Other Poems*. As a Soldiers' Angel, she enjoys volunteering at the Veteran's Administration with monthly food distributions. She and her husband, Steve, live in Decatur, Georgia. They enjoy traveling, cooking together, and spending time with family. With the recent arrival of their first grandchild, they are looking forward to spending lots of time spoiling her.

Frances Johnson Dunston

Frances Johnson Dunston is a retired Pediatrician, public health, and academic medicine leader. She served, usually as *the first* Director of Public Health in Richmond, VA, NJ Commissioner of Health, Associate Dean at the New Jersey Medical School, and Chairperson of Pediatrics at Morehouse School of Medicine. Her most valued achievements include building effective community health programs and facilitating the careers of young health professionals. In her retirement, she has continued her passion for learning and giving back. She is the proud mother of George and Karla and grandmother of Tristan. She has authored her soon-to-be-published memoir, *Beyond Expectations*, about experiencing and overcoming tragic personal loss and rising to live life to its fullest.

Joyce Coleman Edwards

Joyce Edwards is a Project Manager with EY Technology Ernst & Young LLP. Joyce brings a wealth of professional experience, having worked in public, private, and governmental sectors as well as nonprofit and major corporations. As a business administrator, her skill set includes administration, marketing, entrepreneurial technical assistance, and project management. She is an active Leadership Atlanta alumnus and First Congregational Church member, serving as a Deacon. She likes to read and is a Turning Leaf Book Club member. She and her husband, Johnny L. Edwards, a local architect, have been married for 28 years and have traveled the world together. They have three sons and five grandchildren.

Nina R. Hickson

Nina R. Hickson is a mother, daughter, sister, friend, and advocate. She is a proud alumnus of Howard University, where she earned her undergraduate degree in journalism. Ms. Hickson has practiced law for 35 years in various capacities, with her most gratifying position being that of Chief Presiding Judge for Fulton County (GA.) Juvenile Court. During her service to the Court, she met her daughter, Wesley Victoria, who changed her life forever.

Lolita Browning Jackson

Lolita Browning Jackson is a communications strategist who built her professional career around four key pillars - Connecting, Communicating, Collaborating, and Consensus Building- discovering the pillars coexisting with her personal life. Thus, she founded Four Cs Consulting, an external affairs agency specializing in public relations, government, and community affairs. Lolita's an award-winning journalist and business leader who believes in the power of public service for the greater good and fulfills her civic and philanthropic duties while intentionally serving the community. She and her siblings founded the Marie H. Browning Foundation, which, named for their late mother, awards scholarships to students in Brownsville, TN. Lolita earned an

MBA from Clark Atlanta University and a B.S. in Mass Communications from the University of Tennessee at Martin. She resides in Atlanta, Georgia, with her husband, Michael, and son, Aaron.

Roberta Jackson

Roberta Jackson resides outside of Atlanta, GA. She is a proud Atlanta native and a true Georgia Peach. Currently, her occupation is Church Administrative Assistant. She is married to Tyrone, has two sons, Tommie and Isaac and grandchildren, Jordan and Amari. Amari is a *Rainbow Baby*; they are blessings from God! Roberta has a heart for service and outreach projects. In her spare time, she enjoys participating in and watching sports, hidden objects /differences games, riding her bicycle, driving on the open highway, traveling, listening to music, writing, and spending time with her family, especially her grandchildren. She is a published author of *Scenario Queen: God is Omnipresent and Omnipotent; He Never Slumbers or Fail* and *Inspirational Writings from The Creator.*

Tisa Jackson

Tisa Jackson is the branch manager for Wolf Creek Library, a part of the Fulton County Library System. She is a career librarian who loves programming for the communities she serves and collaborating with organizations that help libraries flourish. Her favorite role as a librarian was that of a children's librarian. Tisa is working on a children's story titled *Sujin's Secret* about a little girl with alopecia. Tisa is married and has two sons, one daughter, and a smart, precocious grandson named Tai. Tisa enjoys listening to all genres of music and reading historical African-American stories. Tisa also started a blog that deals with alopecia (www.tresslesstisa.com).

Rosalyn Roberts Mack

Rosalyn Roberts Mack is a retired corporate executive with 34 years of experience in sales, marketing, project management, and business leadership. She earned a B.S. in Chemical Engineering at Howard University and an MBA from Rutgers

University. She has served over nine years as an ordained deacon at First Congregational Church, UCC, Atlanta, GA. Since retiring in 2013, she was called to provide caregiver support for family members. In her spare time, she loves attending OLLI continuing education courses, writing, exercising, attending live music shows, and traveling globally with her husband, Trentton, of over 32 years. They have two adult children, Victoria and Joshua. She and her husband live in Amelia Island, FL, and enjoy hosting family and friends on Amelia Island and in Roswell, GA.

Beatrice Hunter Pack

Beatrice Pack is a life coach, wife, mother, and grandmother who welcomes the calling. She enjoys assisting people in addressing their fears and worries about feeling stuck. She is drawn to individuals, especially the misunderstood, and believes that "everyone has a story" about coming to terms with themselves. Her motto is "*kindness before judgment*." Beatrice retired from a 43-year career; she managed sales, marketing, and business innovation teams and was educated at Central Michigan University. Beatrice is known for her hospitality; she is a health-conscious foodie and enjoys the hunt in shopping. However, her core is community service to those in need, prayer, and family travel. She resides in the Midwest with her husband Rod.

E. Paulette Smith-Epps

E. Paulette Smith-Epps, a native Atlantan, is the daughter of a Baptist minister and an educator. She grew up in Atlanta with three brothers. She received her education from Atlanta Public School System, Spelman College, and Atlanta University. Paulette is a Professional Librarian who was Assistant Director of Public Services when she retired from the Atlanta-Fulton Library System. Currently, she works as a Media paraprofessional in an elementary school. She is a member of St. Paul's Episcopal Church in Atlanta, Georgia, where she is a lay reader. She enjoys singing, listening to music, reading, writing, and traveling the world. Paulette is the mother of three children. She has four grandchildren and four godchildren. Paulette is the widow of William Given Epps, Sr., and lives and works in Atlanta, Georgia.

Gail Tusan Washington

Gail Tusan Washington is a Senior Superior Courts Judge, arbitrator, and mediator with the national dispute resolution company, JAMS. Writing under the pen name Susan Washington, she has published two novels, *Misjudged and Riley, The Judge's Son*. Gail enjoys facilitating creative collaboratives, so the Loving Wisdom anthologies were born. She also serves as the founder and board president of The Pave Foundation, Inc. This nonprofit entity encourages Black girls to "dream in STEAM" through its signature summer enrichment camp, annual Super Science Day of the Girl, and other enrichment activities. Visit www.thepavefoundation.org.

Gail and her husband live in Atlanta with Sammie, their loyal canine rescue. Their most precious moments are spent together with their four adult children and two grandchildren. Learn more about Gail at www.gailtusanwashinton.com.